WASTING TIME

URBAN OUTFITTERS **NICOTEXT**

DO NOT DRINK AND DRIVE & DO NOT DRINK ALCOHOL
IF YOU ARE UNDER DRINKING AGE!

...AND KIDS, REMEMBER, ALWAYS WEAR A CONDOM!

Copyright © NICOTEXT 2007 All rights reserved.
NICOTEXT part of Cladd media ltd.
ISBN: 978-91-85869-26-8
Printed in Canada

Foreword

Wasting time - is there anything better?!

We have all got 24 hours a day to spend the way we want to. Far too much of that time is spent doing boring chores, like working jobs we do NOT like, listening to people bla-bla-ing about stuff we do NOT want to hear, standing in line, or just floating around in some sort of vacuum. Time should be treated better than that. Opposite of what many people may think, there is nothing wrong with wasting time. In fact, a lot of the time, the moments we are the happiest are when we are wasting time. So, go out there, waste some time, be happy and smile at the world - and the world will smile at you.

THIS IS ME

NAME:

THEY CALL ME:

WHAT I DO:

BUT I'D LIKE TO:

MY BEST FEATURE:

NOBODY KNOWS THAT I CAN:

ONE DAY I'LL BE FAMOUS BECAUSE:

FAVORITE JOKE:

I REALLY WANT TO LIVE IN:

I NEED TO BUY NEW:

WHEN I'M HUNGRY, I EAT:

WHEN I'M THIRSTY, I DRINK:

WHEN I'M SAD, I LISTEN TO:

WHEN I'M HAPPY, I LISTEN TO:

THIS IS ME

I ONCE:

WHAT I WOULD MOST LIKE TO SET ON FIRE:

SUPERPOWER I WISH I HAD:

IF YOU WANT TO GET A HOLD OF ME,
YOU'LL MOST LIKELY FIND ME AT:

OR THE:

WHAT I THINK OF ME:

NEXT SUMMER I'LL BE:

I WANT THIS FOR CHRISTMAS:

IF I WERE A PLANT, I'D BE A:

ONE YEAR FROM NOW I WILL HAVE CHANGED THIS:

USELESS FACTS

KNOW EVERYTHING ABOUT ANYTHING – AND MORE.

Women shoplift four times more often than men.

U.S. Presidents who died on July 4th: John Adams and Thomas Jefferson (both in 1826), James Monroe (in 1831).

The microwave was invented after a researcher walked by a radar tube and a chocolate bar melted in his pocket.

Certain frogs can be frozen solid, then thawed, and continue living.

The dial tone of a normal telephone is in the key of "F."

In 1963, baseball pitcher Gaylord Perry remarked, "They'll put a man on the moon before I hit a home run." On July 20, 1969, Gaylord Perry hit his first and only home run, a few hours after Neil Armstrong set foot on the moon.

First novel ever written on a typewriter: Tom Sawyer.

The longest recorded flight of a chicken is thirteen seconds.

Each king in a deck of playing cards represents a great king from history. Spades = King David, Clubs = Alexander the Great, Hearts = Charlemagne, and Diamonds = Julius Caesar.

USELESS FACTS

KNOW EVERYTHING ABOUT ANYTHING – AND MORE.

If a statue of a person on a horse has both front legs in the air, the person died in battle; if the horse has one front leg in the air, the person died as a result of wounds received in battle; if the horse has all four legs on the ground, the person died of natural causes.

Average number of people airborne over the U.S. any given hour: 61,000.

City with the most Rolls Royces per capita: Hong Kong.

America's first nudist organization was founded in 1929 – by three men.

The average bank teller loses about $250 every year.

A lump of pure gold the size of a matchbox can be flattened into a sheet the size of a tennis court.

The only rock that floats in water is pumice.

A pineapple is a berry.

The plant life in the oceans make up about 85% of all the greenery on Earth.

MONUMENTS

KNOW YOUR MONUMENTS.

The Pyramids of Giza	Cambodia
The Taj Mahal	Rio - Brazil
The Statue of Liberty	New York - USA
The Golden Gate Bridge	Rome - Italy
Colosseum	China
The Great Wall	Paris - France
Ayers Rock	Australia
Machu Picchu	Peru
The Eiffel Tower	Paris - France
The Louvre	Moscow - Russia
Big Ben	London - England
Red Square	Rome - Italy
The Parthenon	Arizona / Nevada - USA
The Brandenburg Gate	South Dakota - USA
Manneken Pis	Washington, D.C. - USA
The Leaning Tower	Paris - France
Versailles	Giza - Egypt
The White House	Pisa - Italy
Mount Rushmore	Brussels - Belgium
The Hoover Dam	Berlin - Germany
The Sistine Chapel	Athens - Greece
Christ the Redeemer	San Fransisco - USA
Angkor Wat	India
Stonehenge	England

QUOTES

CONNECT THE PERSON AND THE QUOTE.

Mark Twain:

Thomas Jefferson:

Julius Caesar:

Groucho Marx:

Albert Einstein:

Woody Allen:

William Shakespeare:

Muhammad Ali:

J.C. Penney:

1: "Give me a stock clerk with a goal and I'll give you a man who will make history. Give me a man with no goals and I'll give you a stock clerk."

2: "Put your hand on a hot stove for a minute, and it seems like an hour. Sit with a pretty girl for an hour, and it seems like a minute. THAT'S relativity."

3: "It's not that I'm afraid to die. I just don't want to be there when it happens."

4: "We know what we are, but know not what we may become."

5: "I figured that if I said it enough, I would convince the world that I really was the greatest."

6: "I am a great believer in luck, and I find the harder I work the more I have of it."

7: "Outside of a dog, a book is man's best friend. Inside of a dog it's too dark to read."

8: "Let us be thankful for the fools. But for them the rest of us could not succeed."

9: "I came, I saw, I conquered."

ALI

THE WORLD'S GREATEST FIGHTER.

Born Cassius Marcellus Clay in 1942.

Wins Olympic gold medal in 1960.

In 1964 he becomes world heavyweight champion by defeating Sonny Liston. He defended his title nine times.

Before retiring in 1981, Muhammad Ali compiled a 56–5 record and was the only man to ever win the heavyweight crown three times.

His fights with Joe Frazier and George Foreman were among boxing's biggest events.

Ali has been referred to as "The Louisville Lip", because of his way of speaking about his opponents before a match.

"Float like a butterfly, sting like a bee."

ALI

QUOTES FROM THE GREATEST.

"Service to others is the rent you pay for your room here on earth."

"It's just a job. Grass grows, birds fly, waves pound the sand.
I beat people up."

"I know where I'm going and I know the truth and I don't have to
be what you want me to be. I'm free to be what I want."

"I ain't got no quarrel with those Vietcong."

"I'm so mean I make medicine sick."

"The man who views the world at 50 the same as he
did at 20 has wasted 30 years of his life."

"I'll beat him so bad he'll need a shoehorn to put his hat on."

"I'm not the greatest; I'm the double greatest.
Not only do I knock 'em out, I pick the round."

"People don't realize what they had till it's gone.
Like President Kennedy – nobody like him.
Like The Beatles, there will never be anything like them.
Like my man, Elvis Presley – I was the Elvis of boxing."

SUPER POWERS

YOU'RE A SUPER HERO. CHOOSE TWO SUPER POWERS.

X-Ray vision

Super strength

Super speed

Ability to climb and stick to buildings and walls

Ability to fly

Ability to breathe under water and control sea creatures

Super agility

Ability to freeze things, and control and make ice

Super hearing

Computer wizard

Bat radar sense

Super stretchy-ness

Invisibility

Ability to shoot blasts of fire

Laser vision

Super shrinking power

Cosmic power

Control of all molecules

Ability to communicate with animals

Bull's eye aim

Invulnerability to injury

SUPER POWERS

YOU NEVER KNOW WHAT WILL HAPPEN WHEN YOU WAKE UP TOMORROW...

Teleportation power

Martial arts master

Control thunder and lightning

Control wind and storms

Inhuman shouting power

Skin as hard as steel plates

Ability to shapeshift

Magic and sorcery power

ESP

Control of black magic and voodoo

Mind control

Time travel

Elastic body

Ability to read others' minds

Ability to levitate – yourself and objects

Photographic memory

Can run at supersonic speed

Ability to heal instantly

Ability to freeze things with your breath

Ability to manipulate lottery numbers

FILM

PLAY THE MOVIE GAME!
CONNECT THE ACTOR TO THE MOVIE.

ACTOR	FILM
Tom Hanks	*Say Anything*
Arnold Schwarzenegger	*When Harry Met Sally*
Bill Murray	*The Hitcher*
Tom Selleck	*Reality Bites*
Johnny Depp	*Don Juan DeMarco*
Nicolas Cage	*Con Air*
Nicole Kidman	*Moulin Rouge!*
Julia Roberts	*Conspiracy Theory*
Keanu Reeves	*L.A. Confidential*
Jim Carrey	*Forrest Gump*
Neve Campbell	*Risky Business*
Tom Cruise	*Man on the Moon*
Richard Gere	*Bill & Ted's Excellent Adventure*
Kim Basinger	*Scream*
Christina Ricci	*An Officer and a Gentleman*
Leonardo DiCaprio	*L.A. Story*
Winona Ryder	*The Addams Family*
Rutger Hauer	*Three Men and a Baby*
Steve Martin	*Groundhog Day*
Meg Ryan	*Catch Me If You Can*
John Cusack	*Twins*

BOOK SCRIPT

**EVERYBODY HAS AN IDEA FOR A BESTSELLER.
WRITE YOURS DOWN!**

Title: Genre:

Characters: Leading role:

Where: When:

Plot outline:

Story:

Ending:

ZOMBIES

Zombies are a very real phenomenon typically associated with the voodoo-practicing West Indian country of Haiti. Zombies are people who have died but are not really dead; they are alive, in a state of being referred to as the "undead".

Evil sorcerers called "bokors" bring their victims back to a zombie state of life – a weird half-life where the zombie is incapable of thinking for itself and has no prior knowledge as to whom it was. The bokors then take their victims to remote areas where they are put to work as slaves.

The whole idea of zombies is so ingrained in the psyche of the locals that even the poorest of peasants are willing to pay quite large amounts of money to have heavy slabs placed on the coffins of their loved ones. This practice is thought to deter the bokors.

An American biologist, Wade Davis, suspected that some mysterious substances were used in zombification and he set about to find what they were. He discovered two noteworthy candidates:

– A chemical obtained from pufferfish, called tetrodotoxin, which is an effective nerve poison that can induce deep paralysis.

– A fluid secreted by the skin glands of the highly-poisonous cane toad (Bufo marinus), which is an effective hallucinogen and strong anaesthetic.

ZOMBIES

VOODOO HOODOO – I PUT A SPELL ON YOU!

Other drugs, such as 'zombie cucumber' (*Datura stramonium*), were thought to aid in the resuscitation and mind control of the victim.

It was also found that if persons that had been paralyzed using these drugs were left in their coffins too long, the effects of the mind-controlling zombie cucumber were enhanced due to oxygen starvation, creating irreversible brain damage.

The idea of a zombie as a rotting corpse brought back to life possibly has more to do with the work of novels and movies. But the idea of zombies as drugged individuals, pronounced dead and then buried alive in a coffin awaiting complete brainwashing, appears to hold more truth.

When a man attempted to siphon gasoline from a motor home parked on a Seattle, WA street, he got much more than he bargained for. Police arrived at the scene to find an ill man curled up next to a motor home near spilled sewage. A police spokesman said that the man admitted to trying to steal the gasoline and plugged his hose into the motor home's sewage tank by mistake. The owner of the vehicle declined to press charges, saying that it was the best laugh he'd ever had.

A man walked into a Circle-K in Louisiana, put a $20 bill on the counter and asked for change. When the clerk opened the cash drawer, the man pulled a gun and asked for all the cash in the register, which the clerk promptly provided. The man took the cash from the clerk and fled, leaving the $20 bill on the counter. The total amount of cash he got from the drawer was $15. Question: If someone points a gun at you and gives you money, is a crime committed?

A guy wearing pantyhose on his face tried to rob a store in a mall. When the security guards came, he quickly grabbed a shopping bag and pretended to be shopping, forgetting that he was still wearing the pantyhose. He was captured, and his loot was returned to the store.

MATH

=

THE WORLDS TOUGHEST MATH PROBLEM.

SOLVE THIS AND COLLECT $1 MILLION!

The Riemann Hypothesis

Some numbers have the special property that they cannot be expressed as the product of two smaller numbers, e.g., 2, 3, 5, 7, etc. Such numbers are called prime numbers, and they play an important role, both in pure mathematics and its applications. The distribution of such prime numbers among all natural numbers does not follow any regular pattern. However, the German mathematician G.F.B. Riemann (1826 - 1866) observed that the frequency of prime numbers is very closely related to the behavior of an elaborate function,

$$Z(s) = 1 + 1/2s + 1/3s + 1/4s + ...$$

called the Riemann Zeta function. The Riemann hypothesis asserts that all interesting solutions of the equation,

$$Z(s) = 0$$

lie on a certain vertical straight line. This hypothesis has been checked for the first 1,500,000,000 solutions. A proof that it is true for every interesting solution would shed light on many of the mysteries surrounding the distribution of prime numbers.

Send solution to: Clay Mathematics Institute
One Bow Street Cambridge, Massachusetts 02138 USA

AIRPORTS

KNOW YOUR AIRPORTS!
CONNECT THE AIRPORT TO ITS CITY.

Oslo	Tribhuvan
London	Fiumicino
Tokyo	McCarran
New York	Arlanda
Las Vegas	Heathrow
Toronto	Barajas
Sydney	John F. Kennedy
Buenos Aires	Ezeiza
Lima	J. Chavez
Nairobi	Pearson
Johannesburg	Kingsford
Paris	De Gaulle
Amsterdam	Schiphol
Moscow	Jomo
Reykjavik	Lanseria
Stockholm	Sheremetyvo
Rome	Keflavik
Madrid	Gardermoen
Kathmandu	Narita

FILM

KNOW YOUR MOVIE QUOTES!
WHICH MOVIE DO THESE QUOTES COME FROM?

Scarface   *Sudden Impact*
Dr. No   *Jaws*
Goodfellas   *Star Wars*
A Few Good Men   *Taxi Driver*
Terminator   *The Blues Brothers*
The Godfather   *Gone with the Wind*
Reservoir Dogs

1. "My name is Bond, James Bond."
2. "You can't handle the truth!"
3. "May the force be with you."
4. "Say hello to my little friend."
5. "Whaddaya mean I'm funny? Funny how? Am I a clown? Do I amuse you?"
6. "I'll be back."
7. "I'm gonna make him an offer he can't refuse."
8. "Frankly, my dear, I don't give a damn."
9. "Go ahead, make my day."
10. "You talkin' to me?"
11. "We're on a mission from God."
12. "We're gonna need a bigger boat."
13. "Are you gonna bark all day, little dog, or are you gonna bite?"

URBAN LEGENDS

**TRUTH OR LEGEND? LEGEND OR TRUTH?
EITHER WAY, IT'S A SCARY DATE.**

A boy and a girl are sitting in a parked car in Naval Hill, a favorite parking place for young couples on dates. The car radio is playing romantic music, and the night is warm with promise.

Suddenly a news flash interrupts the music. A lunatic has escaped from a nearby mental hospital, and was last seen in the Naval Hill area. He can be recognized by the gruesome hook, which he has in place of a hand.

The girl is nervous, but the boy doesn't want to leave. She protests but he only kisses her harder.

She reaches out and switches off the radio.

Then they hear a sound of a scratch on the door. Terrified, the girl insists that they leave.

The boy is furious, but he pulls away with a squeal of the tires. At home, he goes around to the passenger door to open it for her and promptly passes out. There, hanging from the door handle, is the bloody stump of the lunatic's hook.

DREAM

WRITE DOWN YOUR MOST RECENT DREAM.
"IT WAS IN A ROOM FILLED WITH CANDY AND PURPLE BALLOONS..."

ELVIS

FACTS AND FIGURES ABOUT "THE KING."
BET YOU DIDN'T KNOW THIS !

Elvis Presley received a Special Agent badge for the Bureau of Narcotics and Dangerous Drugs from President Richard Nixon.

Shoe size: 11D.

Elvis owned 18 TVs, including one installed on the ceiling over his bed.

Elvis was thrown out of the Grand Ole Opry in 1954.

The last food that Elvis Presley ate was four scoops of ice cream and 6 chocolate chip cookies.

In the 1960's Elvis was spending $100 a week on groceries. He also had Pepsi delivered by the truckload.

January 14, 1973, Elvis performed his spectacular "Aloha from Hawaii" live via satellite – the first global show ever broadcast. Over one billion people watched the show, more than watched Neil Armstrong walk on the moon.

ELVIS

**FACTS AND FIGURES ABOUT "THE KING."
BET YOU DIDN'T KNOW THIS!**

Elvis Presley wore a cross, a Star of David, and the Hebrew chai (the symbol for God). He explained his jewelry habit with, "I don't want to miss out on heaven due to a technicality."

Elvis made only one television commercial – an ad for Southern Maid Doughnuts – that ran in 1954.

Elvis carried his own silverware everywhere he went.

Elvis had a pet monkey named Scatters.

Elvis used to be a truck driver, earning $1.25 an hour. His real ambition, however, was to become an electrician. He started evening classes to gain the necessary skills.

Elvis had to pay for his first song recording – forking out a fee of around $4. He wanted to record to hear what his voice sounded like.

Aside from three concerts in Canada, Elvis never performed outside the United States.

(June 1999) On Lake Isabella, in the high desert east of Bakersfield, CA, a woman was having trouble with her boat.

No matter how she tried, the woman just couldn't get her new 22-foot Bayliner to perform. It was sluggish in every maneuver, regardless of what she did. She tried for an hour to make her boat go, but finally gave up and putted over to a nearby marina for help.

A topside check revealed that everything was in perfect working order. The engine ran fine, the outboard motor pivoted up and down, and the prop was the correct size and pitch.

One of the marina guys jumped in the water to check beneath the boat.

When he came up for air, he was laughing so hard he was almost choking on the water.

He had found the problem: under the boat, still strapped securely in place, was the trailer.

THIS IS YOUR LIFE

...AND IT'S ENDING ONE MINUTE AT A TIME.

Average male lifespan: 77 years   Average female lifespan: 82 years

Average time spent sleeping: 25 years and 8 months

Average time spent kissing: 2 whole weeks

Average time spent working: 9 years

Average time spent waiting at traffic lights: 2 weeks

Average time spent watching TV or videos: 5 years and 10 months

Average time spent raising kids and cleaning the house:
Men: 6 years and 8 months
Women: 10 years

Average time spent eating: 5 years and 7 months

Average time spent having sex: 8 months and 1 week

Average time spent getting ready in the mornings:
Men: 1 year and 2 months
Women: 1 year and 5 months

Average time spent exercising:
Men: 2 years, 8 months and 4 weeks
Women: 1 year and 31 days

STUPID INVENTIONS **?**

**WHAT ABOUT A PEANUT BUTTER HAT?
JUST STICK IT ON YOUR HEAD AND EAT ALL DAY!**

On July 6, 1869, C. Singer patented a rocking chair with built-in air conditioning. When the chair rocked, it compressed a big sack of air, which forced air through a pipe and blew it onto the customer's face.

On June 7, 1959, Dexter C. Slater patented a dog-powered engine. The dog generated power by walking on a circular plate, which could be connected to various tools.

On September 18, 1917, C.F. Pidgin patented inflatable tubes to be held in the mouths of silent movie actors. The idea was to write the actors' lines on the tubes, thus making it look like they were saying them.

On February 20, 1900, Ludwig Ederer patented a bed with a built in alarm clock. When it was time to get up, the bed was simply tipped over at a 45 degree angle, and flipped the person sleeping in it to the floor.

On September 19, 1899, Richard Straube patented a rocking chair-bath tub. His goal was to make it even more comfortable to take a bath.

STUPID INVENTIONS **?**

DOCTOR SNUGGLES.

On October 15, 1918, Tony Salari patented a rescue pod for airplanes. The round vehicle was covered with large coils that was supposed to ensure a soft landing.

On September 1, 1855, John O. Lose patented a bicycle with only one wheel. It was also equipped with an umbrella for extra comfort.

On January 29, 1884, La Fayette Wilson Page patented a device for the locomotive. It was a water gun mounted on the very front, that was suppposed to scare wild animals away from the train tracks.

Send your patent to:
United States Patent and Trademark Office
Commissioner for Patents
P.O. Box 1450
Alexandria, VA 22313-1450

ICE CREAM

ICE CREAM FLAVORS.
DON'T WAIT 'TIL SUMMER – CHOOSE 10 FAVORITES NOW!

Vanilla
Dutch Chocolate
Black Cherry
Mint Chocolate Chip
Rum Raisin
Pecan Fudge
English Toffee
Cappuccino Coffee
Maple Walnut
Banana Caramel Ripple
Apple Pie
Strawberry
Raspberry Ripple
Ginger Honey
Grand Marnier & Orange
Honeycomb
Tropical Coconut
Brownie
Bubble Gum
Butter Pecan
Butterscotch
Caramel
Chocolate
Cookie Dough
Cotton Candy
French Vanilla
Grapenut
Chocolate Almond

Maple
Mocha Fudge
Orange Pineapple
Oreo Cookie
Pralines 'n Cream
Rocky Road
Strawberry Cheesecake
Bailey's
Apple Pie & Custard
Ferrero Rocher
Cointreau & Orange
Toffee Fudge
Raspberry Cream
White Chocolate Chip
Forest Fruit
Mocha
Liquorice & Black Currant
Old Fashioned Butter Pecan
Chocolate Chip Cookie Dough
Pistachio Almond
Almond Fudge
Nutty Coconut
Tiramisu
Stracciatella
Lemon-Lime
Vanilla Brownie
Caramelita Caramel

PICK-UP-LINES

A SURE WAY TO COME ACROSS AS A NERD.

- "Am I dead, angel? Cause this must be heaven!"
- "Bond. James Bond."
- "Do you have a map? I just keep on getting lost in your eyes."
- "Hello, I'm a thief, and I'm here to steal your heart."
- "I have only three months to live…"
- "Wouldn't we look cute on a wedding cake together?"
- "Was you father an alien? Because there's nothing else like you on earth!"
- "Stand still so I can pick you up!"
- "Is there an airport nearby or is that just my heart taking off?"
- "If I followed you home, would you keep me?"
- "Your legs must be tired because you've been running around in my mind all night."
- "Your daddy must be a hunter because he sure caught a fox!"
- "If you were a laser, you'd be set on 'stunning'."
- "Excuse me, but you have a beep on your nose." (Reach up and gently squeeze her nose) "BEEP!"
- "Hi, the voices in my head told me to come over and talk to you."
- "I'd marry your cat just to get in the family."
- "If you were a booger I'd pick you first."
- "Pardon me, have you seen my missing Nobel Prize around here anywhere?"

WEIRD FOODS OF THE WORLD

AND YOU THOUGHT CHOPPED LIVER WAS WEIRD. IN SOME COUNTRIES THEY EAT THIS!

Sea Slugs
(Korea)

Jellyfish
(China)

Fish Heads
(Philippines)

Fermented Shark
(Iceland)

Fish Eyes
(Southeast Asia)

Fish Flotation Bladder
(China)

Jellied Eels
(England)

Cod Tongue
(Canada)

Goose Grease
(Germany)

Duck Feet
(China)

Owl Soup
(China)

Song Birds
(Italy)

Chicken heads
(Philippines)

Monkey Toes
(Indonesia)

Pig Blood
(Hungary)

Squirrel Brain
(U.S. - South)

Rat
(Thailand)

Jellied Cow Feet
(Poland)

Sheep Head
(Norway)

Horse Sashimi
(Japan)

Blood Sausage
(Europe)

Bats (Indonesia)

Bull Penis (Asia)

Camel Tendons
(China)

Turtle Eggs
(Nicaragua)

Snake
(China)

Scorpion
(Vietnam)

Tarantula
(Cambodia)

Mopane Caterpillars
(Africa)

Fried Crickets
(Philippines)

Silkworm Grubs
(Korea)

PERSONAL PIZZA

USE YOUR NUMBERS – PICK 8 TOPPINGS!

Your phone-number starts with:

On what date were you born:

How old are you (older than 30, just add the digits together):

How many siblings do you have:

12 + 12 =

What is your shoe size:

How many seconds can you hold your breath (over 30, just add the digits together):

Your weight, divided by 2. Add your age, then multiply by 2. Now add the digits together:

1. Eggs
2. Mayonnaise
3. Peanuts
4. Squid
5. Chocolate
6. Blue Cheese
7. Salmon
8. Ketchup
9. French Fries
10. Marshmallows
11. Oranges
12. Raisins
13. Peas
14. Blueberries
15. Vanilla Ice Cream
16. Shrimp
17. Chicken Liver
18. Rice
19. Corn Flakes
20. Watermelon
21. Onion
22. Cellery
23. Sausage
24. Grapefruit
25. Mustard
26. Cod Liver Oil
27. Bean Sprouts
28. Prunes
29. Macadamia Nuts
30. Soy Sauce

Next time I order pizza, I SWEAR it will have the following toppings:

VAMPIRES

COUNT DRACULA, NOSFERATU, DINGBATS....

Vampires are mythical creatures who try to avoid their own death and demise by literally sucking out the blood out of their victims.

There is much anecdotal evidence to support the existence of vampires, but yet there appears to be no physical evidence of it.

The fear of vampires has been around for a very long time.
Indeed, there are a number of countries, such as Bulgaria, Russia and Greece, where vampire lore may have gotten its start.

If you find yourself being attacked by a vampire, this is how you kill him – and keep him dead:

>>>

VAMPIRES

IF YOU SEE A VAMPIRE, YOUR BEST BET IS TO NOTIFY THE PROPER AUTHORITIES.

- pierce the vampire's heart with a stake,
- expose the vampire to sunlight,
- fill the his corpse with garlic,
- bury him at a four-way crossroads,
- sever the head and cremate the remains,
- form a cross with the arms over the chest, and
- entwine thorny vines over the corpse to ensure it cannot walk again.

The symbol of the cross is also supposed to help to repel vampires, although it will not kill them.

Vampire movies:

- *The Lost Boys*
- *Interview with the Vampire*
- *Dracula*
- *Buffy the Vampire Slayer*
- *Nosferatu*
- *Vampires*
- *Razor Blade Smile*
- *Dracula: Dead and Loving It*
- *Salem's Lot*
- *Return to Salem's Lot*
- *From Dusk Till Dawn*
- *Kindred: The Embraced*
- *Fright Night*

ONE-HIT-WONDERS

HAVE YOU SEEN ANY OF THESE ARTISTS LATELY?
NEITHER HAVE WE.

Nothing Compares 2 U – Sinéad O'Connor
We're Not Gonna Take It – Twisted Sister
Groove is in the Heart – Deee-Lite
The Hustle – Van McCoy
Baby Got Back – Sir Mix-a-Lot
You Light Up My Life – Debby Boone
99 Luftballons – Nena
Rico Suave – Gerardo
Take on Me – A-ha
Ice Ice Baby – Vanilla Ice
Who Let the Dogs Out – Baha Men
I'm Too Sexy – Right Said Fred
Come On Eileen – Dexys Midnight Runners
Tainted Love – Soft Cell
Macarena – Los Del Rio
Kung Fu Fighting – Carl Douglas
Whoomp! (There It Is) – Tag Team
I Want Candy – Bow Wow Wow
What's Up – 4 Non Blondes
Electric Avenue – Eddy Grant
Barbie Girl – Aqua
Spirit in the Sky – Norman Greenbaum
You Gotta Be – Des'ree
Puttin' on the Ritz – Taco
Mmm Mmm Mmm Mmm – Crash Test Dummies
You Get What You Give – New Radicals
We Don't Have To Take Our Clothes Off – Jermaine Stewart
Mambo #5 – Lou Bega
Maniac – Michael Sembello
How Bizarre – OMC

ONE-HIT-WONDERS

...AND THE LIST GOES ON AND ON AND ON AND ON AND ON.

Jump Around – House Of Pain
The Future's So Bright, I Gotta Wear Shades – Timbuk 3
Round and Round – Ratt
More, More, More – Andrea True Connection
867-5309 (Jenny) – Tommy Tutone
What is Love – Haddaway
Smokin' In the Boy's Room – Brownsville Station
It's Raining Men – The Weather Girls
I'm Gonna Be (500 Miles) – The Proclaimers
I Touch Myself – The Divinyls
Turn the Beat Around – Vicki Sue Robinson
True – Spandau Ballet
Rock and Roll (Part 2) – Gary Glitter
Don't Worry, Be Happy – Bobby McFerrin
Rock Me Amadeus – Falco
Hot Child in the City – Nick Gilder
Relax – Frankie Goes to Hollywood
Bitter Sweet Symphony – The Verve
Turning Japanese – The Vapors
Bitch – Meredith Brooks
Afternoon Delight – Starland Vocal Band
Hot Hot Hot – Buster Poindexter
Unbelieveable – EMF
Seasons in the Sun – Terry Jacks
Pass the Dutchie – Musical Youth
It Takes Two – Rob Base & DJ E-Z Rock
All My Life (K-Ci & Jojo) – Sybersound
Play That Funky Music – Wild Cherry
Funkytown – Lipps Inc.
A Girl Like You – Edwyn Collins

HISTORY – EARTH AND MAN

NOW YOU CAN SKIP READING THAT THICK HISTORY BOOK OF YOURS.

12 billion years ago: A very Big Bang

12 billion years ago: 3 minutes later: nuclei form

12 billion years ago: Atoms after 300,000 years

4.6 billion years ago: Milky Way and the sun

4.6 billion years ago: Nuclear dust becomes solar system

4.5 billion years ago: Earth condenses as hot solid sphere

4 billion years ago: Earth's surface becomes rock and water

3.5 billion years ago: First life on earth appears (bacteria)

3 billion years ago: Algae in water

1 billion years ago: Sponges and jellyfish in sea

500 million years ago: Fishes have skeletons

400 million years ago: Plants move to land

350 million years ago: Insects take flight

340 million years ago: Amphibians get lungs

300 million years ago: Reptiles rule

250 million years ago: Earth has only one continent (Pangaea)

225 million years ago: Dinosaurs inherit the earth

225 million years ago: Birds appear on the scene

200 million years ago: Single continent begins to crumble

170 million years ago: First tiny mammals evolve

HISTORY – EARTH AND MAN

EVERYTHING SHOULD BE THIS EASY!

65 million years ago: Dinosaurs die out

65 million years ago: Mammals in many forms

50 million years ago: Australia becomes 'down under'

45 million years ago: Primates living in the trees

20 million years ago: Ancestors of apes swing from branches

15 million years ago: Large primates like living on the ground

4 million years ago: Apes walk tall

4 million years ago: Some primates seem quite human

3 million years ago: "Lucy" lives in Ethiopia

2 million years ago: First humans in east Africa

2 million years ago: Humans chip stones for tools

1,8 million years ago: Our first direct ancestor

1,7 million years ago: Chilly times ahead (Ice Age)

1 million years ago: Humans move into Asia and Europe

1 million years ago: Origins of speech

500,000 years ago: "Beijing man" tries cave living

500,000 years ago: Fire invented

250,000 years ago: German elephant stabbed with spear

230,000 years ago: Neanderthal Man

150,000 years ago: Second migration from Africa?

90,000 years ago: First glimpse of modern man

DANCE LESSON

DO THE CHA-CHA – DANCE LESSONS.

WHO KNOWS WHEN YOU MIGHT BE INVITED TO A CHA-CHA PARTY NEXT. YOU'D BETTER START PRACTICING THOSE STEPS...

The Cha-Cha came from the Cuban Mambo. It originated during the Mid-1950s when musicians began syncopating the fourth beat of music which resulted in a "triple step." Dancers soon began creating steps based on this new triple step pattern and the resulting dance became known as the Triple Mambo. Now it is called the Cha-Cha.

A bit faster than the Cuban Rumba, the Cha-Cha emphasizes staccato movements and incorporates limitless syncopations making it a dynamic and exciting dance.

Face your partner, close your feet and stand on your Right Foot (RF).

Face your partner, close your feet and stand on your Left Foot (LF).

DANCE LESSON

CHA-CHA-CHA-CHA-CHA-CHA-CHA-CHA-CHA.
IT'S REALLY FUNNY IF YOU SAY IT OVER AND OVER AGAIN!

1
Step onto your LF (Slow)

1
Step onto your RF (Slow)

2
Step onto your RF (Slow)

2
Step onto your LF (Slow)

3
Step onto your LF (Slow)

3
Step onto your RF (Slow)

4
Step onto your RF (Quick)

4
Step onto your LF (Quick)

5
Step onto your LF (Quick)

5
Step onto your RF (Quick)

6
Step onto your RF (Slow)

6
Step onto your LF (Slow)

7
Step onto your LF (Slow)

7
Step onto your RF (Slow)

8
Step onto your RF (Slow)

8
Step onto your LF (Slow)

9
Step onto your LF (Quick)

9
Step onto your RF (Quick)

10
Step onto your RF (Quick)

10
Step onto your LF (Quick)

URBAN LEGENDS

**TRUTH OR LEGEND?
THE LUMP IN THE RUG.**

A carpet-layer has just finished installing wall-to-wall carpeting in a home. But as he is standing back admiring the job and patting his pockets looking for his cigarettes, he notices a lump in the middle of the floor. He does not find the cigarettes in his pocket, so he concludes that he must have dropped them while he was working and rolled the new carpet right over them.

He is not about to remove the new carpet just for a packet of cigarettes, so he takes a hammer from his tool box and pounds down the lump, neatly flattening it. As he puts his tools into his truck, he notices his cigarettes lying there on the dashboard. Just then the lady of the house comes out and asks, "Did you by any chance see my hamster while you were working? It got out of its cage again."

URBAN LEGENDS

TRUTH OR LEGEND?
NICE DOGGY.

A woman from La Mesa, CA, went to Tijuana, Mexico, to do some shopping. As any visitor to this border town knows, the streets near the shopping areas are populated with stray dogs. The woman took pity on one little stray and offered it a few bites of her lunch, after which it followed her around for the rest of the afternoon.

When it came time to return home, the woman had become so attached to her little friend that she couldn't bear to leave him behind. Knowing that it was illegal to bring a dog across the international border, she hid him among some packages on the seat of her car and managed to pass through the border checkpoint without incident. After arriving home, she gave the dog a bath, brushed his fur, then retired for the night with her newfound pet curled up at the foot of her bed.

When she awoke the next morning, the woman noticed that there was an oozing mucus around the dog's eyes and a slight foaming at the mouth. Afraid that the dog might be sick, she rushed him to a nearby veterinarian and returned home to await word on her pet's condition.

The call soon came. "I have just one question," said the vet. "Where did you get this dog?" The woman didn't want to get into trouble, so she told the vet that she had found the dog running loose in the street near her home in La Mesa. But the vet didn't buy it. "You didn't find this dog in La Mesa. Where did you get it?"

The woman nervously admitted having brought the dog across the border from Tijuana. "But tell me, doctor," she said. "What is wrong with my dog?"

His reply was brief and to the point. "First of all, it's not a dog, it's a Mexican sewer rat. And second, it's dying."

MARILYN MONROE

PO-PO-PI-DO!
OR WAS THAT BETTY BOOP? WE DON'T KNOW, BUT IT SURE SOUNDS NEAT!

Birth name: Norma Jean Mortenson, baptized Baker, changes her name to Marilyn Monroe in 1956.

Born: June 1, 1926, Los Angeles, CA.

Died: August 5, 1962, age 36, Los Angeles, CA.

Marilyn was once voted "The girl most likely to melt Alaska."

Marilyn appeared on 36 magazine covers in one year.

Marilyn was sewn into her infamous "Happy Birthday, Mr. President" dress.

Marilyn was crowned the first "Artichoke Queen" in 1947 for the Artichoke Festival, in Castroville, CA.

Marilyn was paid only $50 for the most famous nude photo of all time.

MARILYN MONROE

FAMOUS QUOTES FROM THE MOST POPULAR BLOND IN THE WORLD.

"An actress is not a machine, but they treat you like a machine. A money machine."

"Hollywood is a place where they'll pay you a thousand dollars for a kiss and fifty cents for your soul."

"I don't mind living in a man's world as long as I can be a woman in it."

"It's not true that I had nothing on. I had the radio on."

"The body is meant to be seen, not all covered up."

"I don't know who invented high heels, but all women owe him a lot."

"If I'd observed all the rules, I'd never have got anywhere."

BOOKS

1984	James Joyce
The Adventures of Huckleberry Finn	Jacqueline Susan
Catch-22	Umberto Eco
The Catcher in the Rye	Paul Auster
Wuthering Heights	John Steinbeck
Moby Dick	Harper Lee
Lord of the Flies	Robert Louis Stevenson
Great Expectations	Jane Austen
Don Quixote	Hunter S. Thompson
The Old Man and the Sea	George Orwell
Fear and Loathing in Las Vegas	Ernest Hemingway
Pride and Prejudice	Miguel de Cervantes
Treasure Island	Charles Dickens
To Kill a Mockingbird	William Golding
The Grapes of Wrath	Herman Melville
The New York Trilogy	Emily Brontë
The Name of the Rose	J.D. Salinger
Valley of the Dolls	Joseph Heller
Generation X	Mark Twain
Ulysses	Douglas Coupland
Charlie and the Chocolate Factory	Roald Dahl

SITCOMS

WHO'S WHO IN SITCOMS?
CONNECT THE CHARACTER AND THE SITCOM.

Jerry	*Sabrina the Teenage Witch*
Homer	*Friends*
Phoebe Buffay	*Home Improvement*
Al Bundy	*Everybody Loves Raymond*
Cartman	*Roseanne*
Niles Crane	*Futurama*
Bender	*The Cosby Show*
Fez	*Spin City*
Dharma	*Will and Grace*
Will Smith	*Cheers*
Sam Malone	*Seinfeld*
Jack McFarland	*The Fresh Prince of Bel-Air*
Paul Lassiter	*Dharma and Greg*
Heathcliff Huxtable	*That 70's show*
Dan Conner	*Frasier*
Robert Barone	*Southpark*
Dr. John 'J.D.' Dorian	*Married... with Children*
Sabrina Spellman	*Scrubs*
Tim Taylor	*The Simpsons*

RIDDLES

EVIL DWARF

You are on your way to visit your grandmother on her birthday. Since it's such a nice, sunny day you decided to walk there. You are carrying a box of chocolates and flowers for granny. Halfway there, you come to an intersection. One road goes to the left, the other to the right.

You scratch your head, unsure which way is the right one. There's no one to ask, except a dwarf standing in the middle of the intersection. The dwarf knows the right way to granny, but he'll only permit one question. For every other question you ask, he'll lie to you.

What one question can you ask so you can find out which road to take?

RIDDLES

ARAB SHEIKH CAMELS

An old Arab sheikh must will his fortune to only one of his two sons. He makes a proposition: his two sons will ride their camels in a race, and the one whose camel crosses the finish line last will win the fortune.

During the race, the two brothers wander aimlessly for days, neither willing to cross the finish line. In desperation, they ask a wise man for advice. When he responds, both brothers leap onto their camels and charge toward the finish line.

What did the wise man say?

HOURGLASSES

You have two hourglasses: a 7-minute one and an 11-minute one. How can you accurately time 15 minutes using only these two hourglasses?

STARING CONTEST

PRACTICE YOUR STARING SKILLS.
NO BLINKING. NO LAUGHING.

STARING CONTEST

PRACTICE YOUR STARING SKILLS.
NO BLINKING. NO LAUGHING.

THE HISTORY OF...

CHEWING GUM

Thomas Adams began experimenting with chicle as a substitute for rubber. Adams tried to make toys, masks, and rain boots out of chicle, but every experiment failed. Sitting in his workshop one day, tired and discouraged, he popped a piece of surplus stock into his mouth. Chewing away, the idea suddenly hit him to add flavoring to the chicle. Shortly after, he opened the world's first chewing gum factory. By the early 1900s, improved methods of manufacturing, packaging and marketing, put modern chewing gum well on its way to its current popularity.

According to the *Guinness Book of World Records* the biggest bubble ever was 22 inches diameter – 1 1/2 times the size of a large pizza.

Only two percent of North American fourth-graders can blow a "double bubble" – a bubble inside a bubble.

A "triple whammy" is a bubble inside a bubble inside a bubble.

Chewing gum burns about 11 calories per hour.

THE HISTORY OF...

THE FRISBEE

A baker named William Russel Frisbie, of Warren, CT, came up with a clever marketing idea back in the 1870s. He put his family name in relief on the bottom of the light tin pans in which his company's homemade pies were sold. The pans were reusable, but Frisbie hoped that every time a housewife started to bake a pie in one, she would see the name Frisbie and think, "How much easier to buy one".

During the 1940s, students began sailing the pie tins through the air and catching them. A decade later, a flying-saucer enthusiast in California named Walter Frederick Morrison designed a saucer-like disk for playing catch. It was produced by a company named Wham-O. On a promotional tour of college campuses, the president of Wham-O encountered the pie-plate-tossing craze at Yale. And so the flying saucer from California was renamed after the pie plate from Connecticut. The name was changed from Frisbie to Frisbee to avoid any legal problems.

ALIEN

WHAT DO ALIENS LOOK LIKE?
DRAW A PICTURE NEXT TIME YOU SEE ONE.

ALIEN:

THE ALIEN'S SPACESHIP:

DRAW

MAKE YOUR OWN PAINTING.
JUST FOLLOW THESE SIMPLE INSTRUCTIONS.

YOUR NAME

SUN

CASTLE

MONKEY

CLOUDS

TITS

FLOWER

CAR

OINK OINK

**BEEN TO A FARM LATELY?
KNOW YOUR ANIMAL SOUNDS.**

Sss Sss	Duck
Oink Oink	Snake
Bzzzz	Dove
Meow	Donkey
Moo	Turkey
Woof	Bee
Hee-Haw	Cat
Quack Quack	Sheep
Baah	Cow
Hoot Hoot	Chicken
Gobble Gobble	Dog
Coo Coo	Pig
Peep Peep	Owl

EMERGENCY

THIS IS IMPORTANT STUFF.

CALL

 CALL 911!

BLOW

 TILT HEAD, LIFT CHIN, CHECK BREATHING.

 **GIVE TWO BREATHS.**

PUMP

 **POSITION HANDS IN THE CENTER OF THE CHEST.**

 FIRMLY PUSH DOWN TWO INCHES ON THE CHEST 15 TIMES.

CONTINUE WITH TWO BREATHS AND 15 PUMPS UNTIL HELP ARRIVES

PHOBIAS

EVERYBODY'S SCARED OF SNAKES AND HEIGHTS, BUT CHECK OUT THESE SCAREDY-CATS!

Abluthophobia:	Fear of bathing
Acousticophobia:	Fear of noise
Aeronausiphobia:	Fear of vomiting due to airsickness
Anthrophobia:	Fear of flowers
Ballistophobia:	Fear of missles or bullets
Brontophobia:	Fear of thunder storms
Cacomorphobia:	Fear of fat people
Cathisophobia:	Fear of sitting
Chinophobia:	Fear of snow
Chrometophobia:	Fear of money
Dentophobia:	Fear of dentists
Dinophobia:	Fear of whirlpools
Eisoptrophobia:	Fear of mirrors
Entomophobia:	Fear of insects
Ergophobia:	Fear of work
Felinophobia:	Fear of cats
Galeophobia:	Fear of sharks
Gallophobia:	Fear of France or the French
Heliophobia:	Fear of the sun

PHOBIAS

SCAREDY-CAT SCAREDY-CAT SCAREDY-CAT SCAREDY-CAT!!!

Hippophobia:	Fear of horses
Ideophobia:	Fear of ideas
Japanophobia:	Fear of Japanese
Lilapsophobia:	Fear of tornadoes
Lunaphobia:	Fear of the moon
Macrophobia:	Fear of long waits
Melissophobia:	Fear of bees
Nephophobia:	Fear of clouds
Novercaphobia:	Fear of your mother-in-law
Papaphobia:	Fear of the Pope
Phobophobia:	Fear of phobias
Pogonophobia:	Fear of beards
Sciophobia:	Fear of shadow
Siderophobia:	Fear of stars
Siderodromophobia:	Fear of train travel
Theatrophobia:	Fear of theatres
Teutophobia:	Fear of Germany or Germans
Verbophobia:	Fear of words
Xanthophobia:	Fear of the color yellow

RIDDLES

RIDDLE ME THIS, RIDDLE ME THAT, WHO'S AFRAID OF THE BIG, BLACK BAT?

CORK, BOTTLE, COIN

If you were to put a coin in an empty bottle and then insert a cork in the bottle's opening, how could you remove the coin without taking out the cork or breaking the bottle?

KNIGHT VS. DRAGON

A dragon and knight live on an island. This island has seven poisoned wells, numbered one to seven. If you drink from a well, you can only save yourself by drinking from a higher numbered well. Well number seven is located at the top of a high mountain, so only the dragon can reach it.

One day, they decide that the island isn't big enough for the two of them, and they have a duel. Each of them brings a glass of water to the duel, They exchange glasses, and drink. After the duel, the knight lives and the dragon dies.

Why did the knight live? Why did the dragon die?

(May 2001) In a poorly judged attempt to convince his wife that he was sober enough to drive, a 29-year-old man pulled up to a state police barracks in his pickup truck, parked illegally, and demanded a sobriety check. He failed the Breathalyzer test and was taken into custody. "Basically," an amused Sergeant Paul Slevinski explained, "his wife won the argument."

(July 1999) In Marathon Beach, FL, a guy was fishing with his buddies when he saw fins in the water. "Dolphins!" he thought, and jumped into the water to swim with the dolphins. Surprise! The fins turned out to belong to sharks. His buddies fished him out of the ocean, and Mr. One-With-Nature was treated at a local hospital for shark bites.

(Jan 2001) A Charleston, WV, man got into hot water when he claimed to be buying heroin in another state as an alibi for a bank robbery. He gave the police a hotel receipt and they searched room – where they found 84 packets of heroin. Police decline to comment on the man's fate.

BEATLES

READ ALL ABOUT THE MUSIC MANIACS OF THE CENTURY!

After Paul McCartney's song, "Penny Lane" became a Beatles hit, the street signs for the actual Penny Lane in Liverpool disappeared with such regularity (as they did on the real Abbey Road) that the town reverted to simply painting 'Penny Lane' on the buildings, rather than have street signs.

The Beatles had numerous inspirations for their name. Stuart Sutcliffe noted that a motorcycle gang in the film, *The Wild One*, was called 'The Beetles,' and John Lennon reportedly had a dream in which a man appeared "on a flaming pie," saying, "You will be Beatles with an 'a'." The band members were also influenced by the name of Buddy Holly's band, The Crickets.

On December 17, 1963, a disc jockey at WWDC in Washington, D.C., became the first person to broadcast a Beatles record on American airwaves. James Carroll played "I Want To Hold Your Hand," which he had got from his stewardess girlfriend who gave it to him when she brought the single back from England. Due to listener demand, it played daily, every hour. Since it hadn't been released yet in the states, Capitol initially considered court action, but instead released the record earlier than planned.

Though she bought him his first guitar, John Lennon said his Aunt Mimi discouraged him from a career in music, saying: "The guitar's all right as a hobby, but it won't earn you any money." Years later, John gave her a silver plaque with that quote engraved upon it.

BEATLES

FAMOUS QUOTES FROM THE BIGGEST BASTARDS ON EARTH.

"If everyone demanded peace instead of another television set, then there'd be peace."
– John Lennon

Reporter: What do you call that hairstyle you're wearing?
George Harrison: Arthur.

"You have to be a bastard to make it, and that's a fact. And the Beatles are the biggest bastards on earth."

"We thought that if we lasted for two to three years that would be fantastic."

"Life is what happens to you when you're busy making other plans."

"As far as I'm concerned, there won't be a Beatles reunion as long as John Lennon remains dead."

"Would those of you in the cheaper seats clap your hands? And the rest of you, if you'll just rattle your jewelry."

Reporter: How did you find America?
John Lennon: Just turn left at Greenland.

USELESS FACTS

KNOW EVERYTHING ABOUT EVERYTHING.

By the time a child finishes elementary school, she will have witnessed 8,000 murders and 100,000 acts of violence on television.

C3P0 is the first character to speak in *Star Wars*.

Chocolate syrup was used for blood in the famous shower scene in Alfred Hitchcock's movie, *Psycho*. The scene, which lasted 45 seconds, actually took seven days to shoot.

Disneyland opened in 1955.

Donald Duck lives at 1313 Webfoot Walk, Duckburg, Calisota.

Gunsmoke debuted on CBS in 1955 and went on to become the longest-running series on television. It was on the air for 20 years.

In 1920, 57% of Hollywood movies billed the female star above the leading man. In 1990, only 18% gave the leading lady top billing.

In 1938 Joe Shuster and Jerry Siegel sold the rights to the comic-strip character Superman to their publishers for $130.

USELESS FACTS

KNOW EVERYTHING ABOUT EVERYTHING – AND MORE.

In October 1959, Elizabeth Taylor became the first Hollywood star to receive $1 million for a single picture (*Cleopatra*).

Movie detective Dirty Harry's badge number is 2211.

MTV made its debut at 12:01 a.m. on August 1, 1981. The first music video shown on the channel was, appropriately, "Video Killed the Radio Star" by the Buggles. MTV's five original VJ's were Martha Quinn, Nina Blackwood, Mark Goodman, J.J. Jackson and Alan Hunter.

The first Academy Awards were presented in 1927.

The first time the "f" word was spoken in a movie was by Marianne Faithfull in the 1968 film, *I'll Never Forget Whatshisname*. In Brian De Palma's 1984 movie, *Scarface*, the word is spoken 206 times – an average of once every 29 seconds.

The characters Bert and Ernie on Sesame Street were named after Bert the cop and Ernie the taxi driver in Frank Capra's *Its A Wonderful Life*.

The song "Happy Birthday to You" was originally written by sisters Mildred and Patty Hill as "Good Morning to You." The words were changed and it was published in 1935.

WEREWOLVES

Werewolves are creatures that are said to turn from humans into wolves.

During the Dark Ages, Europe's population lived in very real fear of werewolves. The signs that were used to determine whether or not someone was a werewolf included:

- hairy hands or feet,

- small and pointed ears that were usually quite low and towards the back of the head,

- thick eyebrows that meet in the middle,

- protruding teeth,

- red-tinged, curled fingernails,

- long third fingers,

- drinking at wolves' watering holes,

- eating wolves and wolf brains, and

- persons being killed by wolves.

If you know anyone fitting in on this description, stay away from them during the full moon!

WEREWOLVES

MORE HOWLIN' AT THE MOON.

Hollywood has helped to add a few characteristics of its own to the legend of the werewolf. Many werewolf films suggest that a full moon is the trigger for a person to change into a wolf. They also suggest that a werewolf bite may turn you into a werewolf.

Do you have a werewolf problem where you live? Shooting the animal with blessed silver bullets, are said to be a deterrent for these creatures.

Werewolf movies:

- *Van Helsing*
- *An American Werewolf in Paris*
- *Wolf*
- *Silver Bullet*
- *An American Werewolf in London*
- *The Howling*
- *The Curse of the Werewolf*
- *The Wolf Man*

YELLOW CAB

ALMOST AS FUN AS A YELLOW SUBMARINE.

Of the 42,000 cabbies in New York City, 82% are foreign-born. Twenty-three percent are from the Caribbean (the Dominican Republic and Haiti), and 20% are from South Asia (India, Pakistan, and Bangladesh).

The yellow taxi was popularized by John D. Hertz, who started the Yellow Cab Company in 1915. Hertz painted his cabs yellow after he read a study identifying yellow as the most visible color from long distances.

There are more than 13,000 taxis operating in New York, not including over 40,000 other for-hire vehicles.

Safety tip: When you get our of a cab, always do so through the door closest to the sidewalk!

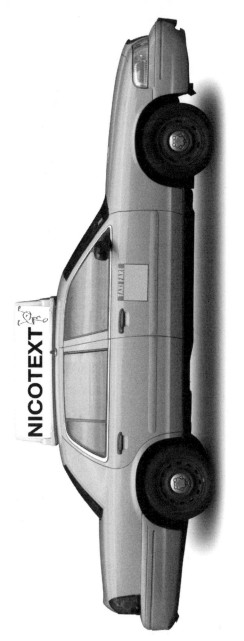

NICOTEXT

SO YOU ALWAYS HAVE ONE...

1. Personal
(Anything about your personality or body you'd like to improve.)

2. Material
(Stuff you want – money, cars, a boyfriend etc.)

3. Humane
(For the greater good – world peace, food for the hungry etc.)

PRESENTS

FREDERICK GETS A GERMAN SHEPERD, CARL GETS A DVD,
MOM GETS A NEW MERCEDES AND DADDY GETS A SILK TIE .
PLAN AHEAD FOR BIRTHDAYS AND CHRISTMAS.

PRESENT: TO: OCCASION:

VAGABOND

TRAVEL THE WORLD.
X = PLACES YOU'VE BEEN, O = PLACES YOU'RE GOING

A
Afghanistan
Albania
Algeria
Andorra
Angola
Antigua and Barbuda
Argentina
Armenia
Australia
Austria
Azerbaijan

B
Bahamas, The
Bahrain
Bangladesh
Barbados
Belarus
Belgium
Belize
Benin
Bhutan
Bolivia
Bosnia and Herzegovina
Botswana
Brazil
Brunei
Bulgaria
Burkina Faso
Burma (Myanmar)
Burundi

C
Cambodia
Cameroon
Canada
Cape Verde
Central African Republic
Chad
Chile

China
Colombia
Comoros
Congo
Costa Rica
Côte d'Ivoire
Croatia
Cuba
Cyprus
Czech Republic

D
Denmark
Djibouti
Dominica
Dominican Republic

E
East Timor
Ecuador
Egypt
El Salvador
England (U.K.)
Equatorial Guinea
Eritrea
Estonia
Ethiopia

F
Fiji
Finland
France

G
Gabon
Gambia
Georgia
Germany
Ghana
Great Britain (U.K.)

Greece
Grenada
Guatemala
Guinea
Guinea-Bissau
Guyana

H
Haiti
Honduras
Hungary

I
Iceland
India
Indonesia
Iran
Iraq
Ireland
Israel
Italy

J
Jamaica
Japan
Jordan

K
Kazakhstan
Kenya
Kiribati
Korea, North
Korea, South
Kuwait
Kyrgyzstan

L
Laos
Latvia
Lebanon

VAGABOND

TRAVEL THE WORLD.
X = PLACES YOU'VE BEEN, O = PLACES YOU'RE GOING

Lesotho
Liberia
Libya
Liechtenstein
Lithuania
Luxembourg

M
Macedonia
Madagascar
Malawi
Malaysia
Maldives
Mali
Malta
Marshall Islands
Mauritania
Mauritius
Mexico
Micronesia
Moldova
Monaco
Mongolia
Montenegro
Morocco
Mozambique
Myanmar

N
Namibia
Nauru
Nepal
Netherlands, The
New Zealand
Nicaragua
Niger
Nigeria
Northern Ireland (U.K.)
Norway

O
Oman

P
Pakistan
Palau
Panama
Papua New Guinea
Paraguay
Peru
Philippines, The
Poland
Portugal

Q
Qatar

R
Romania
Russia
Rwanda

S
St. Kitts and Nevis
St. Lucia
St. Vincent and The Grenadines
Samoa
San Marino
São Tomé and Príncipe
Saudi Arabia
Scotland (U.K.)
Senegal
Serbia
Seychelles
Sierra Leone
Singapore
Slovakia
Slovenia
Solomon Islands, The
Somalia
South Africa
Spain
Sri Lanka
Sudan
Suriname
Swaziland

Sweden
Switzerland
Syria

T
Taiwan
Tajikistan
Tanzania
Thailand
Togo
Tonga
Trinidad and Tobago
Tunisia
Turkey
Turkmenistan
Tuvalu

U
Uganda
Ukraine
United Arab Emirates
United Kingdom
United States
Uruguay
Uzbekistan

V
Vanuatu
Vatican City
Venezuela
Vietnam

W
Wales (U.K.)
Western Sahara

Y
Yemen

Z
Zaire
Zambia

WALT DISNEY ★

HE CREATED A NEW WORLD.

Walt Disney only attended one year of high school.

In 1923, Walt and Roy formed the Disney Brothers Studio in California. At Roy's insistence, the company soon became the Walt Disney Studio, since he felt that Walt's name should be emphasized. This date is officially recognized as the starting date of The Walt Disney Company.

Walt grew his famous mustache at age 25.

He was the voice of Mickey Mouse for two decades.

He often ate lunch at his desk – his favorite meal was chili and beans, which he ate with tomato juice and soda crackers.

He admitted to being "scared to death" when he had to face the camera to introduce episodes of the "Disneyland" television series.

He won more Oscars than anyone else – 32 of them.

Disney is actually a changed version of Walt's family's original name. The original family name was D'Isigny.

His first motion picture was a 1928 short titled "Steamboat Willie."

When Walt was younger, he was hired to work at *The Kansas City Star* newspaper. He was later fired from the paper because of lack of creativity. Years later, The Disney Company bought ABC, which owned *The Kansas City Star*.

WALT DISNEY

FAMOUS QUOTES FROM THE MOUSE-MAN!

"I only hope that we never lose sight of one thing – that it was all started by a mouse."

"When I started on Disneyland, my wife used to say, 'But why do you want to build an amusement park? They're so dirty.' I told her that was just the point – mine wouldn't be."

"Disneyland is like a piece of clay: If there is something I don't like, I'm not stuck with it. I can reshape and revamp."

"Laughter is America's most important export."

"That's the real trouble with the world – too many people grow up. They forget. They don't remember what it's like to be twelve years old."

"We allow no geniuses around our studio."

"The way to get started is to quit talking and begin doing."

"You're dead if you aim only for kids. Adults are only kids grown up, anyway."

"You reach a point where you don't work for money."

USELESS FACTS

KNOW EVERYTHING ABOUT ANYTHING – AND MORE.

A chimpanzee can learn to recognize itself in a mirror, but a monkey can't.

A rat can last longer without water than a camel can.

Adult cats with no health problems are in deep sleep 15% of the time. They are in light sleep 50% of the time.

Ants don't sleep.

At 188 decibels, the whistle of the blue whale is the loudest sound produced by any animal.

China's Beijing Duck Restaurant can seat 9,000 people at one time.

Fortune cookies were invented in 1916 by George Jung, a Los Angeles noodle maker.

In a room there are three lightbulbs, on the wall. In another room there are three switches. The mean professor will pay you $1 million if you can figure out which switch controls which lightbulb.

The thing is, you can only enter the room with the lightbulbs in it one time. Can you figure it out?

SEX TRIVIA

THIS IS THE REASON THEY INVENTED BABIES.

A pig's orgasm lasts about 30 minutes.

The average man sees five women a day he would like to sleep with.

In 1995, Mo Ka Wang, a Chi Kung master in Hong Kong, lifted over 250 pounds of weight two feet off the floor with his erect penis.

Black women are 50% more likely than white women to have an orgasm when they have sex.

Minks have intercourse that lasts an average of eight hours.

Average number of times a man will ejaculate from masturbation in his lifetime: 2,000.

The largest human vagina belonged to a woman who was 7'8" tall.

Seventy-two percent of men admit to fantasizing about their workmates.

If your sex partner is covered with wet food, you may have a "sploshing" fetish.

POEM TIME

WRITE A POEM USING THE FOLLOWING WORDS.

NUCLEAR PLANT
RED
HEAT
RAINDROPS
TICKLE
NYLON
EYELASHES

WHITE RABBIT
SEA BASS
OCEAN
KEYMASTER
FINLAND
TIME
BLAST

GOOD DEEDS

HEAVEN, HERE I COME!

- ☐ HELP AN OLD LADY ACCROSS THE STREET.
- ☐ HELP A CAT OUT OF A TREE.
- ☐ BUILD AND PUT UP BIRD HOUSES.
- ☐ HELP A SLEEPING HORSE GET UP.
- ☐ PARK CARS FOR CHURCH VISITORS.
- ☐ PICK SPLINTER FROM A DOG'S PAW.
- ☐ STOP CARS AT A SCHOOL CROSSING.
- ☐ PUT OUT A FIRE.
- ☐ PICK UP GARBAGE FROM THE SIDE OF THE ROAD.
- ☐ GUIDE TOURISTS AROUND YOUR HOME TOWN.
- ☐ SERVE SNACKS TO FIREFIGHTERS ON ASSIGNMENT.
- ☐ HELP DIRECT TRAFFIC.
- ☐ FEED BIRDS.
- ☐ PAY PARKING FEES FOR OTHER CARS.
- ☐ BUY FLOWERS FOR YOUR MOTHER.
- ☐ CLEAR SOMEONE'S GARDEN OF WEEDS.

COPY

FOLLOW THE WHITE PEACE SIGN.

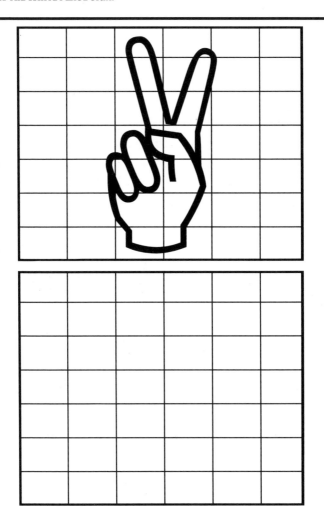

1990's

REMEMBER THE '90'S?
THIS MIGHT HELP YOU ALONG.

The Macarena
During the 1990's, you couldn't turn on the radio or go to parties without hearing this song.

The 'Rachel' Haircut
Many women in the 1990's started cutting their hair in the same style as Jennifer Aniston's character 'Rachel' on the popular television sit-com *Friends*.

Napster
This music-sharing community, which is now a paid service, was once free. All internet users had to do was download the software and they could get any MP3 music file they wanted.

Beanie Babies
As one of the most popular, endearing and widespread fads of the last 25 years, one would imagine that Beanie Babies must have some type of unique and incredible attributes. Instead, they are simply small, inexpensive, stuffed animals with a tag stating the animal's name and birth date.

Fanny Packs
Purses that buckle on to the waist. Very popular in the early 1990.

The 'Wassup' Commerical
This popular beer commercial started a new trend for the '90's. People were answering their own phones and saying, "Wasssssssuuup!!".

1990's

**REMEMBER THE '90'S?
THIS MIGHT HELP YOU ALONG.**

Overalls
In the early 1990's, teens wore their overalls one of two ways: either with a belt, and letting the front flap and back straps hang straight down, or they only hooked together one side of the overall straps, leaving the opposite side open.

Piercings
Getting your tongue, belly button, eyebrow, etc. pierced was *the* popular thing to do to show your coolness.

Tattoos
Formerly only for gang members, jailbirds and other rebels you used to get a tattoo to stand out, now you get one to blend in.

Bleached Hair
This fad was popular with high school and college students. Many just bleached the tips of their hair. This fad really caught on in the mid 90's and continued into 2000.

Tamagotchi
Very popular little electronic device that needed to be fed and cared for. If not, it would die.

Boy Bands
Backstreet Boys | 'N Sync | Take That

Grunge
Whether it was worn-out jeans or a flannel shirt, grunge music and grunge fashion were big in the '90's. So was Nirvana.

SAYINGS

FILL IN THE MISSING WORD.

It ain't over 'til the .... sings.

Misery loves ....

Life in a vacuum cleaner ....

There's a first time for ....

A chain is only as strong as its weakest ....

Better safe than ....

A few sandwiches short of a ....

You can't teach an old dog ....

Making a world of ....

A journey of a thousand miles begins with the first ....

Too little too ....

A man's home is his ....

Pay an arm and a ....

A rolling stone gathers no ....

Out of the ....

All roads lead to ....

Movers and ....

P-A-L-I-N-D-R-O-M-E
E-M-O-R-D-N-I-L-A-P

A WORD, PHRASE, VERSE, OR SENTENCE THAT READS
THE SAME BACKWARDS OR FORWARD.

A MAN, A PLAN, A CANAL: PANAMA.

EMIL, A SLEEPY BABY, PEELS A LIME.

KNOB RED, NO WONDER! BONK.

FLEE TO ME, REMOTE ELF.

RACECAR.

SOLO GIGOLOS.

MAC SPOTS TIP AT A PIT-STOP SCAM.

BAN CAMPUS MOTTO, "BOTTOMS UP, MACNAB."

OH, CAMERAS ARE MACHO.

GARY KNITS A STINKY RAG.

YO, BANANA BOY!

NO, MEL GIBSON IS A CASINO'S BIG LEMON.

U.F.O. TOFU.

HE WON SNOW, EH?

CIGAR? TOSS IT IN A CAN. IT IS SO TRAGIC.

ALBERT EINSTEIN

ALBERT EINSTEIN, A SMART, SMART MAN.

Einstein, Albert (1879-1955): German-born American physicist and Nobel laureate, best known as the creator of the special and general theories of relativity, and for his bold hypothesis concerning the particle nature of light. He is perhaps the most well-known scientist of the 20th century.

$$E=mc2$$

Albert Einstein's brain is preserved, and resides in several bottles at Princeton University.

Albert Einstein was a premature baby. He did not speak until age 3.

Canadian researchers have found that Einstein's brain was 15% larger than the average brain. Scientists at a University in Ontario, Canada have discovered that the part of Einstein's brain thought to be related to mathematical reasoning – the inferior parietal region – was 15% wider on both sides than a normal brain.

ALBERT EINSTEIN

FAMOUS AND VERY, VERY SMART QUOTES!

"Imagination is more important than knowledge."

"Gravitation is not responsible for people falling in love."

"I want to know God's thoughts; the rest are details."

"The hardest thing in the world to understand is the income tax."

"I never think of the future. It comes soon enough."

"Anyone who has never made a mistake has never tried anything new."

"The secret to creativity is knowing how to hide your sources."

"The only thing that interferes with my learning is my education."

"We can't solve problems by using the same kind of thinking we used when we created them."

"Education is what remains after one has forgotten everything he learned in school."

"The important thing is not to stop questioning. Curiosity has its own reason for existing."

Lawnchair Larry

(1982) Larry Walters of Los Angeles, CA, is one of the few to contend for the Darwin Awards and live to tell the tale. "I have fulfilled my 20-year dream," said Walters, a former truck driver for a company that makes TV commercials. "I'm staying on the ground. I've proved the thing works."

Larry's boyhood dream was to fly. But fate conspired to keep him from his dream. He joined the Air Force, but his poor eyesight disqualified him from a job as a pilot. After he was discharged from the military, he sat in his backyard watching jets fly overhead.

He hatched his weather balloon scheme while sitting outside in his "extremely comfortable" Sears lawnchair. He purchased 45 weather balloons from an Army-Navy surplus store, tied them to his tethered lawnchair dubbed the "Inspiration I", and filled the four-foot-diameter balloons with helium. Then, packed up some sandwiches, Miller Lite, and a pellet gun, and strapped himself in. He figured he would pop a few of the many balloons when it was time to descend.

Larry's plan was to sever the anchor and slowly float up to a about 30 feet above his back yard, where he would enjoy a few hours of flight before coming back down. But things didn't work out quite as planned.

When his friends cut the cord anchoring the lawnchair to his Jeep, Larry did not float lazily up to 30 feet. Instead, he streaked into the LA sky as if shot from a cannon, pulled by the lift of 42 helium balloons holding 33 cubic feet of helium each. He didn't level off at 100 feet, nor did he level off at 1000 feet. After climbing and climbing, he leveled off at 16,000 feet.

At that height, Larry felt he couldn't risk shooting any of the balloons, lest he unbalance the load and really find himself in trouble. So he stayed there, drifting cold and frightened, with his beer and sandwiches, for more than 14 hours. He crossed the primary approach corridor of LAX, where TWA and Delta pilots radioed in reports of the strange sight.

Eventually, Larry gathered the nerve to shoot a few balloons, and slowly descended. The hanging tethers tangled and caught in a power line, blacking out a Long Beach neighborhood for 20 minutes. Larry climbed to safety, where he was arrested by waiting members of the LAPD. As he was led away in handcuffs, a reporter dispatched to cover the daring rescue asked him why he had done it. Larry replied nonchalantly, "A man can't just sit around."

The Federal Aviation Administration was not amused. Safety Inspector Neal Savoy said, "We know he broke some part of the Federal Aviation Act, and as soon as we decide which part it is, a charge will be filed."

BERMUDA TRIANGLE

**DO DI DO DO, DO DI DO DO.
(SINGING THE TWILIGHT ZONE THEME.)**

The Bermuda Triangle is also known as the "Devil's Triangle." The area, which is located off the southeastern coast of the United States, bears some resemblance to a triangle. The apexes of the triangle are generally accepted to be Bermuda; Miami, FL; and San Juan, Puerto Rico. The area became infamous because of 'a high incidence of unexplained losses of ships, small boats, and aircraft.' Some of the more famous cases of loss over the area include:

Cyclops
(U.S. Navy collier, vanished in 1918)
The Cyclops, 541 feet long, weighing 19,290 tons and with a crew of 300, is one of the largest ships lost in the Bermuda Triangle. Carrying ore, The Cyclops disappeared without a trace en route from Barbados to the eastern United States. The Cyclops was the first ship, which carried a radio to disappear, but the crew sent no emergency message.

Carroll A. Deering
(Five-masted schooner, found abandoned in 1921)
The Carroll A. Deering left Rio de Janeiro without cargo to return to Norfolk, VA. Several weeks later it was seen by the crew of a lightship, under full sail with the crew all together on the deck. One of the crew shouted that they had lost both anchors. Two days later the ship was found beached on the shore with the sails still set and the lifeboats and crew's belongings on board. But the crew themselves were missing, and were never seen again.

BERMUDA TRIANGLE

DO DI DO DO, DO DI DO DO –
(SINGING THE TWILIGHT ZONE THEME)

Marine Sulphur Queen
(Cargo ship, vanished in 1963)
The Marine Sulphur Queen left Texas carrying a cargo of molten sulphur. When it could not be contacted after failing to send a routine radio message, a search began. Only some debris, including a foghorn and life-jacket, was found.

Flight 19
(Five U.S. Navy bombers and a rescue plane, vanished in 1945)
The case of Flight 19 is the most famous and mysterious of all. There are many different accounts of this case, but the basic facts are that a group of five aircraft vanished at the same time, along with the search plane that was sent to find them.

Star Tiger
(Tudor IV airliner, vanished in 1948)
After flying from the Azores, the British airliner Star Tiger had nearly reached Bermuda when the pilot radioed that the weather was good and that he expected to arrive on time. But the aircraft never arrived, and a search for survivors and wreckage revealed nothing.

Douglas DC-3
(Airliner, vanished in 1948)
This aircraft was flying to Miami, from Puerto Rico. The pilot radioed that he was 50 miles south of the airfield, but soon afterwards the airfield could not get a response from the plane. A search found no sign of the aircraft, even though the water in the area where it disappeared was only 20 feet deep. The DC-3 had simply vanished.

DREAM HOUSE

DRAW A PICTURE OF YOUR DREAM HOUSE.
WHEN YOU'RE RICH, JUST HAND IT OVER TO THE ARCHITECT.

MUSIC HIT

PUT THAT SONG LIVING INSIDE YOU ON PAPER!

Title: Genre:

Story:

First line:

Verse:

Lyrics:

Instrument: Beat:

MOVIE SCRIPT

HOLLYWOOD, HERE I COME! QUENTIN TARANTINO STARTED OUT WORKING AT A VIDEO STORE. ONE DAY HE GOT AN IDEA...

Title: Genre:

Cast: Leading role:

Where: When:

Plot outline:

Story:

Ending:

TO-BUY-LIST

YOU'VE WON $10 MILLION!
MAKE A LIST OF WHAT YOU'RE GOING TO BUY WITH THE MONEY.

PEPTALK

LOVE THYSELF, LOVE OTHERS, LOVE ALL.

YOU CAN DO IT! **YOU CAN DO IT! YOU ARE BEAUTIFUL!**YOU LOOK COOL! **IT WILL FEEL BETTER TOMORROW**YOU ARE RIGHT AND THEY ARE WRONG!

I LOVE YOU! LOVE

YOU ARE THE BEST! YOU ARE FUNNY!YOU ARE THE BEST! YOU ARE FUNNY!YOU ARE THE BEST! YOU ARE FUNNY!YOU ARE THE BEST! YOU ARE FUNNY!YOU ARE THE BEST! YOU ARE FUNNY! I JUST WANT TO KISS YOU!

YOU'RE MY BEST FRIEND!THAT HAT REALLY
SUITS YOU!I WISH I WAS MORE LIKE YOU I WISH I WAS MORE LIKE YOU I WISH I WAS MORE LIKE YOU I WISH I WAS MORE LIKE YOU I WISH I WAS MORE LIKE YOU I WISH

I WAS MORE LIKE YOU I WISH I WAS MORE LIKE YOU I WISH I WAS MORE LIKE YOU I WISH I WAS MORE LIKE YOU I WISH I WAS MORE LIKE YOU I WISH I WAS **MORE LIKE YOU**

I WISH I WAS MORE LIKE YOU! YOU ARE THE SMARTEST **PERSON I KNOW!**
WHERE DO YOU GET IT ALL FROM? WHERE DO YOU GET IT ALL FROM?

I JUST WANT TO KISS YOU!

YOU MAKE ME HAPPY!YOU MAKE ME HAPPY!YOU MAKE ME HAPPY!YOU MAKE ME HAPPY!YOU MAKE ME HAPPY!YOU MAKE ME HAPPY!YOU MAKE

ME HAPPY!YOU MAKE ME HAPPY!YOU ARE A SUPERSTAR!YOU ARE A SUPERSTAR!YOU ARE A SUPERSTAR!YOU ARE A SUPERSTAR!YOU ARE A SUPERSTAR!YOU ARE A SUPERSTAR!YOU ARE A SUPERSTAR!YOU ARE A

SUPERSTAR!**YOU ARE A SUPERSTAR!**

THE WORLD'S FUNNIEST JOKE

HA HA AHHA HA AHHA HA AHHA HA AHHA HA AHHA HA AH
HA HA AHHA HA AHHA HA AHHA HA AHHA HA AHHA HA AHHA HA HA!

The world's funniest joke was unveiled by scientists at the end of the largest study of humor ever undertaken.

For years, people around the world have been invited to judge jokes on a website as well as contribute jokes of their own. The LaughLab experiment conducted by psychologist Dr. Richard Wiseman, from the University of Hertfordshire in England, attracted more than 40,000 jokes and almost two million votes.

Here it is, the world's funniest joke:

Two hunters are out in the woods when one of them collapses. He doesn't seem to be breathing and his eyes are glazed.

The other guy whips out his phone and calls 911. He gasps, "My friend is dead! What can I do?"

The operator says, "Calm down, I can help. First, let's make sure he's dead."

There is a silence, then a shot is heard. Back on the phone, the guy says, "OK, now what?"

Now you can laugh your ass off.

COPY

FOLLOW THE WHITE DOVE.

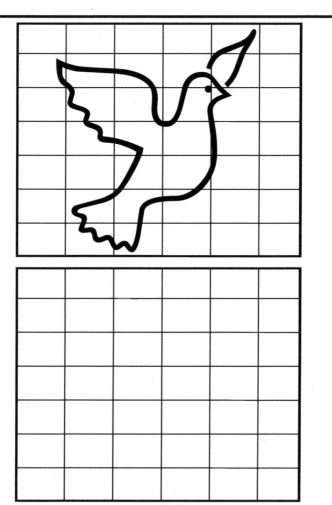

FASHION HISTORY

The first rubber-soled shoes called "plimsolls" were developed and manufactured in the United States in the late 1800s. In 1892, nine small rubber manufacturing companies consolidated to form the U.S. Rubber Company. Among them was the Goodyear Metallic Rubber Shoe Company, organized in the 1840s in Naugatuck, CT.

This company was the first licensee of a new manufacturing process called vulcanization, discovered and patented by Charles Goodyear. Vulcanization uses heat to meld rubber to cloth or other rubber components for a sturdier, more permanent bond.

On January 24, 1899, Humphrey O'Sullivan received the first patent for a rubber heel for shoes.

From 1892 to 1913, the rubber footwear divisions of U.S. Rubber were manufacturing their products under 30 different brand names. The company consolidated these brands under one name. When choosing a name, the initial favorite was Peds, from the Latin meaning foot, but someone else held that trademark. By 1916, the two final alternatives were "Veds" or "Keds", with the stronger-sounding Keds being the final choice.

Keds® were first mass-marketed as canvas-top sneakers in 1917. These were the first sneakers. The word "sneaker" was coined by Henry Nelson McKinney, an advertising agent for N.W. Ayer & Son, because the rubber sole made the shoe stealthy or quiet, all other shoes, with the exception of moccasins, made noise when you walked. In 1979, the Stride Rite Corporation acquired the Keds® brand.

PHONETIC ALPHABETS

AMERICAN POLICE	SPANISH POLICE
Alpha	Antonio
Bravo	Barcelona
Charlie	Carmen
Delta	Chocolate
Echo	Dolores
Foxtrot	Enrique
Golf	Francia
Hotel	Gerona
India	Historia
Juliet	Israel
Kilo	José
Lima	Kilo
Mike	Lorenzo
November	Llobregat
Oscar	Madrid
Papa	Navarra
Quebec	Ñoño
Romeo	Oviedo
Sierra	París
Tango	Quebec
Uniform	Ramón
Victor	Sábado
Whiskey	Tarragona
X-ray	Uruguay
Yankee	Valencia
Zulu	Washington
	Xiquena
	Yegua
	Zaragoza

When you talk into a mobile telephone, it converts the sound of your voice to radio frequency energy (radio waves). The radio waves are transmitted through the air to a nearby base station. The base station then sends the call through the telephone network until it reaches the person you are calling.

When you receive a call on your mobile phone, the message travels through the telephone network until it reaches a base station near to you. The base station sends out radio waves, which are detected by your telephone and converted back to speech. Depending on the equipment and the operator, the frequency that the phone uses is 900MHz, 1800MHz or 2100MHz.

CHOICES

CHOICES, CHOICES.
IF YOU HAD TO CHOOSE, WHICH WOULD YOU RATHER PICK?

Be three feet taller OR be three feet shorter?

Win $500 for yourself OR win $5,000000 for charity?

Have the ability to fly OR have the ability to be invisible?

Have reversed knee joints OR have reversed elbow joints?

Have a foot-long nose OR have a foot-long tongue?

Eat a block of butter OR eat a block of salt?

Spend 4 years in jail for something you never did
                    OR
spend 10 years in jail for something you did do?

Have to say the phrase:
'Tootsie smells better this year' every 10 minutes
                    OR
'Daddy does a mean mambo' every 10 minutes?

Be in a chamber of 100,000 fire ants for a week
                    OR
wear a poison ivy suit for a month?

**DO YOU HAVE AN ANSWER FOR THIS?
IF YOU DO, PLEASE LET US KNOW.**

If a General is a higher ranking officer than a Major,
then why is a major illness worse than a general illness?

Why is it called a soap opera when nobody sings?

If a pack of gum says that each piece is 10 calories,
is that just for chewing the gum, or only if you swallow it?

Why do we say "heads up" when we actually duck?

If there was a crumb on the table and you cut it in half,
would you have two crumbs or two halves of a crumb?

Do stairs go up or down?

If the sky is the limit, then what is space? Over the limit?

When French people swear do they say, "Pardon my English"?

Can you get cornered in a round room?

How come you play at a recital, but recite at a play?

Why do you go "back and forth" if you really
must go forth before you go back?

If something "goes without saying," why do people still say it?

THE HISTORY OF...

THE HAIR DRYER.

The first hair dryer was the vacuum cleaner! Around the turn of the century, women dried their hair by connecting a hose to the exhaust of their vacuum cleaners. In early models, the front of a vacuum cleaner sucked air in, the back blew air out, and the hose could be attached to either end.

In 1920, the first true hair dryer came on the market, but it was extremely large and heavy, and frequently overheated. Not until 1951 was the first really workable hair dryer made.

THE HISTORY OF...

THE POPSICLE.

An 11-year-old named Frank Epperson invented the Popsicle by accident. One day, Frank mixed some soda water powder and water, which was a popular drink in those days. He left the mixture on the back porch overnight with the stirring stick still in it. The temperature dropped to a record low that night and the next day Frank had a stick of frozen soda water to show his friends at school.

Eighteen years later, in 1923, Frank Epperson remembered his frozen soda water mixture and began a business producing Epsicles in seven fruit flavors. The name was later changed to the Popsicle. He realized the commercial possibilities of his invention and applied for a patent, which was granted in 1924. By 1928, Epperson had earned royalties on more than 60 million Popsicle ice pops.

FASHION HISTORY

HISTORY OF THE T-SHIRT.

The days of the T-shirt began during WWI when American American troops noticed European soldiers wearing lightweight cotton undershirts on hot summer days. Compared to wool uniforms, the undershirts were cool and they caught on fast with the Americans. By the 1920's, "T-shirt" became an official word in the American English language with it's inclusion in Merriam-Webster's Dictionary. By WWII, both the Navy and the Army had included T-shirts as standard issue underwear.

John Wayne, Marlon Brando and James Dean all shocked Americans by wearing their underwear on TV. In 1951, Marlon Brando really surprised them when, when his shirt gets ripped off of his body revealing his naked chest.

By 1955, James Dean made T-shirts really cool in *Rebel Without A Cause.*

In the '60's, people began to tie-dye and screen print the basic cotton T-shirt. Advances in printing and dyeing allowed more variety. Tank tops, muscle shirts and other T-shirts followed.

>>>

T-shirts were inexpensive, and in style, and you could make them with any statement you wanted. In the late '60's and '70's. Rock 'n roll bands began to realize that they could make substantial amounts of money selling their T-shirts. Sports caught on to the idea and soon the officially licensed screen-printed T-shirt became hot merchandise.

During the '80's and '90's manufacturing of screen-printed T-shirts increased, and T-shirts were being called a commodity.

Today, printed T-shirts with witty slogans are very popular. You will continue to see T-shirts worn, because they are cool, fun and part of our daily life. T-shirts will still be here when you and I are long gone.

Television personalities have helped increase the popularity recently by wearing them on highly rated programs.

HOW STUFF WORKS

HOW DOES A MICROWAVE WORK?

A miniature radio station or magnetron tube sends microwaves into the oven cavity. Inside the oven they bounce around to give even cooking. Since microwaves bounce off of metal, the oven is a six-sided metal box to keep the waves from escaping.

They pass through plastic or glass, like sunshine goes through a window pane, with no effect at all. Therefore, we cook in vessels made from these materials.

The microwaves don't actually cook the food. Microwaves penetrate food about one inch in all directions (top, bottom, and sides) causing the water molecules to move and vibrate against one another at the rate of 2 1/2 billion times per second.

The heat from the vibrating molecules on the outer edges of the food must go somewhere. It is by "conduction" that heat moves inward, layer by layer, to cook the food.

Microwaves are attracted like magnets to the fat, sugar and water within food. Water molecules are very good absorbers of microwaves, but sugar and fat are better. Salt is the best. Thus, foods high in fat, sugar and salt will cook faster and get hotter than foods made up primarily of water, such as vegetables.

HOW STUFF WORKS

The typical home toilet uses a bowl filled with water to work. When you flush the toilet, it starts a siphon that drains the bowl. Gravity then carries the water into the septic tank or the sewer system.

The problem with this approach on an airplane is that the motion of the vehicle means you cannot use a bowl filled with water – it would splash out every time a little turbulence came along. Since there is no bowl of water, you cannot use a siphon or gravity to empty the bowl.

Instead, airplane toilets use an active vacuum rather than a passive siphon. They are therefore called vacuum toilets. When you flush an airplane toilet, it opens a valve in the sewer line and the vacuum in the line sucks the contents out of the bowl and into a tank. Because the vacuum does all the work, it takes very little water (or the blue sanitizing liquid used in airplanes) to clean the bowl for the next person. Most vacuum systems flush with just half a gallon of fluid or less, compared to 1.6 gallons for a normal toilet.

TALK THE TALK

WHADSA MADDA WID DA WAY NOO YAWKERS TAWK?
IF YA WANNA LERN HOWDA TAWK LYKA NOO YAWKA, YUV KUMTUDA RIGHD PLAYCE!

NEW YORKER	ENGLISH
Assawayigoze	That's the way it goes
Braykidup	Break it up
Domblokadoor	Don't block the door
Doity	Dirty
Dooawg	Dog
Fahcrissake	For Christ's sake
Fuhgeddaboutit	Forget about it
Gwan	Go on
Hootoadjuh	Who told you
Jeet	Did you eat
Kee-ab	Cab
Noo Joisey	New Jersey
Lemmeauf	Let me off
Nyesplayshagottere	Nice place you got here
Shaddup	Shut up
Sowaddyasay	So what do you say
Toe babies	Strawberries
Uf caws	Of course

If all else fails, here's a phrase that works
for every New York situation:

FUCK YOU, YOU FUCKING FUCK!!!

Up your nose with a rubber hose – Go to Hell

Why don't you take a long walk on a short pier? – Why don't you just go away?

Knock the horns off, wipe its ass, and drag it in! – I'd like that steak rare

Your ass is grass and I'm the lawn mower – You are in big trouble

Colder than a witch's tit in the winter – Freezing cold

Busier than a one legged cat tryin' to bury shit on a marble floor – A very busy person

Don't let your mouth write checks your ass can't cash – Don't make promises you can't keep

Meaner than a acre full of wild pussycats – Pretty damn mean

Well, cut off my legs and call me shorty – I'm amazed

Clear as mud – Don't understand what you mean

Let's make like a tree and leave – Time to go

Dumber than a box of rocks – Quite stupid

Hold your horses – Be patient

(July 1999) Ken from Carlsbad, CA, accepted a dare and kissed a snake, landing himself in mortal danger yesterday. Ken proudly bragged to his friends about a deadly young rattlesnake that he had taken into captivity the week before. They teased him by calling him a "snake lover," and they urged, "kiss your girlfriend, Ken."

When he did, the three-foot rattler bit him on the lower lip and pumped its sac of venom into the unfortunate man. His head and throat swelled to two times their normal size, and Emergency Room personnel pumped vial after vial of anti-venom into his bloodstream in a fight for his life.

After three hours of intubation and 25 doses of anti-venom, Ken was out of danger at the Tri-City Medical Center.

The swelling from a snakebite can cause necrosis of the affected tissue, and Ken might have lost part of his face. He was fortunate, and will only see bruised and stretched facial skin in the mirror. But he will suffer the consequences of his foolish act for weeks, as flu-like symptoms set in, caused by an immune response to anti-venom.

Dr. Neil Joebchen said, "In 26 years, this is the worst case I've seen. His muscles were quivering like he had worms under the skin."

Safety tip of the week: Don't play with rattlesnakes – they bite!

HEY, IDIOT!

**TRUE STORIES ABOUT TRUE IDIOTS –
TO GO OUT WITH A BANG.**

(February 1981) Phoenix Field airport in Fair Oaks, CA, had been subject to recurring petty thefts from neighborhood teenagers, so a security firm was retained to patrol the grounds. Thefts decreased sharply, but fuel consumption was on the rise. This puzzling situation continued until late one night, when a passerby noticed a flaming airplane on the field.

By the time the fire department arrived, the plane had completely melted into the tarmac. While the firemen extinguished the residual flames, the passerby noticed a uniformed figure lying facedown several yards away. It was a security guard!

He was revived and questioned.

Turns out, he had been siphoning fuel from small planes to use in his car. The plane he selected that night had a unique fuel storage system involving hollow, baffled wing spars. When the guard shoved the siphon in, it stubbed against the first baffle. No matter how he twisted, pushed, and pulled the hose, he could not siphon any fuel from the plane.

Exasperated, he lit a match to see inside the tank... and the rest is history.

GHOSTS

SPOOKY SPECTERS.

Ghosts are believed to be the spirits of dead people. They are said to appear in bodily likeness to living persons and often haunt their former habitats. Some people believe that ghosts are the souls of the deceased, demons or spirits.

There are four possible solutions as to what constitutes a ghost:

1) a departed spirit,
2) the replay of something that had happened in the past,
3) a malfunction of the mind or hallucination or
4) elementals, divas or gins.

There are literally thousands of ghost stories that have been told over the years. Practically everybody knows somebody who has either heard of a ghost or even seen one. The list below contains some of the different types of ghosts that have been documented over the years.

Biker Ghosts
Crisis Apparition
Deathbed Visions
False Arrival Apparition
Ghostly Transport
Haunting Ghosts
Spectral Battles
Whistling Ghosts

GHOSTS

HAUNTED HOWLIN' CREATURES OF DARKNESS.

Ghost movies:

- *The Changeling*
- *The Innocents*
- *The Others*
- *The Sixth Sense*
- *Don't Look Now*
- *They Watch*
- *The Mothman Prophecies*
- *Vertigo*
- *The Haunting*
- *The Uninvited*
- *Lady in White*
- *The Watcher in the Woods*
- *The Woman in Black*
- *The Canterville Ghost*
- *Thirteen Ghosts*

If you are having troubles with ghosts in your area,
who you gonna call? – GHOSTBUSTERS!!!!!

FASHION HISTORY

THE HISTORY OF THE JEAN.

The Gold Rush of 1848 attracted many adventurers to California. One of them was a 20-year-old named Levi Strauss. Strauss had been a draper, or cloth seller, in New York, and he took a few bolts of cloth to sell on the journey west.

In this manner he earned his way, and by the time he reached California, Levi Strauss had sold everything except a roll of canvas. No one wanted clothes made of canvas! Or did they?

It turned out that "up in the diggings," where the miners worked, pants wore out very quickly. So Strauss made some pairs of canvas trousers to sell to miners. More and more miners were coming to Strauss and asking him for a pair of those canvas trousers.

Not entirely happy with canvas, Levi started using a new fabric from Genoa, Italy. The weavers there called the fabric "genes." Strauss changed the name to "jeans" and later he called his pants "Levi's." They became popular with cowboys as well as miners.

And the rest is history...

COPY

FOLLOW THE WHITE HEART.

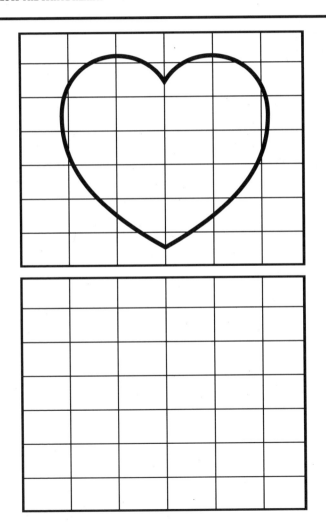

HOW STUFF WORKS

HOW DOES A LIGHTBULB WORK?

There are two types of lightbulbs: incandescent and fluorescent.

An incandescent bulb uses heat caused by an electrical current. When electrical current passes through a wire, it causes the wire to heat. The wire, or filament, gets so hot that it glows and gives off light. Everyday incandescent light bulbs have a filament made of tungsten. Since the hot tungsten would quickly burn away if it were exposed to oxygen, it must be placed in a sealed glass bulb which is either evacuated or filled with a gas that won't let it burn.

Another common type of light is the fluorescent lamp. A fluorescent lamp is a glass tube filled with argon gas and mercury vapor. When electrical current is passed through the gas, the atoms of the gas pick up energy and radiate it in the form of ultra-violet light (and some heat). The UV light then strikes the inside of the tube, which is coated with a phosphor. The phosphor glows, giving off the light we see.

Fluorescent lamps don't require high temperatures to produce light, like incandescent bulbs do. Energy must be used in heating the in-candescent bulb, and a large part of that energy is lost as heat, not light. In the fluorescent lamp, a larger portion of the energy is radi-ated as light.

HOW STUFF WORKS

HOW DOES A RAINBOW WORK?

Rainbows usually occur during or just after a rainstorm once the sun has come back out, but they can occur whenever sunlight passes through water droplets.

Rainbows are caused by the refraction, or bending, of sunlight as it passes through the raindrops, which act like miniature prisms. As white light enters the prism, it is separated into the individual wavelengths of light, which we see as the different colors in a rainbow. Thus the spectrum, or band of colors that make up the "white light," exits the prism as separate bands of color. The more slowly a wavelength of light travels, the more it is bent by the prism. That is why the colors seen in the rainbow are always in the order: red, orange, yellow, green, blue, indigo and violet. The red light travels more slowly than violet light, so it is bent more.

Since rainbows are made by sunlight passing through water droplets, it is possible to create your own miniature rainbow. Spray a fine mist of water in the direction of the sun and watch as the rainbow appears!

At the end of the rainbow lies a burried treasure – usually a box filled with golden coins. Next time you see a rainbow, go look for it.

COPY

FOLLOW THE WHITE SKULL.

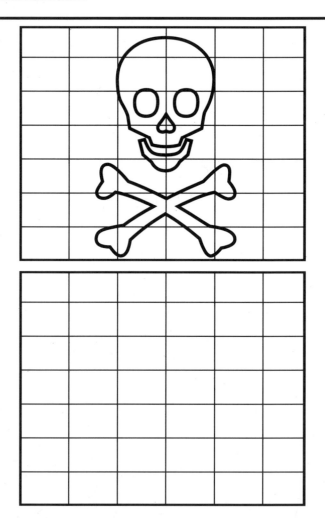

UFO

WHEN THEY COME – FOR THEY WILL COME – BE PREPARED.

Every three minutes a UFO is seen somewhere in the world.

As many as 71% of Americans believe that the government withholds evidence about UFO's.

According to a study made 1991, more than 4 million Americans claimed to have been abducted by aliens.

In the city of Basel, Switzerland, a UFO sighting was reported on August 7, 1566.

The first UFO picture ever taken was shot in Zacatecas, Mexico, by the astrologist José Bonilla.

In April 1897, in Le Roy, KS, Alexander Hamilton reported seeing an airship come down from the sky and kidnap a cow.

The first UFO sighting to be taken seriously by authoritites was made by Winston Churchill, who reported seing a strange airship outside Kent, England in 1912.

On February 25th, 1942, a large, dark object could be seen in the air above Los Angeles. The army first thought it was Japanese fighter planes ready to attack. When they sent up planes to inspect it, they didn't find anything. A report of a possible UFO sighting was sent to President Roosevelt.

All through the 1960's, NASA repeatedly filmed UFOs during their space missions.

UNEXPLAINABLE

WELL, WE JUST CAN'T EXPLAIN IT.

Yeti: A creature usually described as a shaggy man-beast, which is only ever briefly seen moving across snow-swept landscapes, leaving behind very large footprints. The yeti is also known as the Abominable Snowman.

Have you seen a shaggy man-beast in your neighborhood?
Notify the proper authorities.

Alchemy: A medieval chemical philosophy or art, of turning metal into gold.

Atlantis: According to Plato (428 - 348 B.C.), Atlantis was believed to be a vast island continent, situated to the west of the Pillars of Hercules (the straits of Gibraltar). In Plato's books *Timaeus* and *Critias*, he wrote of a highly-advanced civilization (similar to that of Atland), which inhabited Atlantis. Unfortunately, within a single day and due to very violent storms and earthquakes, both the island continent of Atlantis and its highly advanced inhabitants were destroyed. It is believed that the whole continent simply sank to the bottom of the sea.

The source of Plato's information was an Athenian scholar called Solon, who in turn had learned of Atlantis from long-lost priests and archives whilst visiting Egypt around 600 B.C.

To this day no one is really sure about the exact geographical location of Atlantis, although many theories have been put forward regarding this over the years. The research continues.

UNEXPLAINABLE

WELL, WE JUST CAN'T EXPLAIN IT.

Weeping Statues: Satues that have the ability to display certain aspects of human behavior, such as crying or bleeding. There have also been reports of paintings that can exhibit this unusual phenomenon. Although this phenomenon is not exclusive to the Catholic Church, most of its reports in the past have tended to originate from Catholic countries in Europe. An example of a weeping statue is contained in the following newspaper report:

A six-inch-high porcelain statue began weeping tears of blood. The liquid staining the image is genuinely blood, and human at that. The Santiago coroner's office pronounced the substance is type 0 – human blood. The statue weeps regularly, particularly in the presence of children.

It was confirmed by doctors attached to the police Criminal Investigation Department that the mysterious red liquid, which flows from the eyes of a statue of the Virgin Mary belonging to a Chilean woman, is indeed human blood. It was stated by Dr. Inelia Chacon that three samples of the liquid examined in a laboratory were shown to be blood.

The small, blue and white porcelain statue belongs to Olga Rodriguez, a housewife from the working class La Cisterna district in the south of Santiago. Since 14 November, when the tears of blood were seen for the first time, the modest home of Mrs. Rodriguez has become the main attraction for residents of the district. The Church has refused to take up a position concerning this strange phenomenon.

Honeybees use nectar to make honey. Nectar is almost 80% water, with some complex sugars. The bees use their long, tubelike tongues like straws to suck the nectar out of the flowers and they store it in their "honey stomachs."

Bees actually have two stomachs – a honey stomach, which they use like a nectar backpack, and their regular stomach. The honey stomach holds almost 70 mg of nectar, and when full, it weighs almost as much as the bee does. Honeybees must visit between 100 and 1500 flowers in order to fill their honey stomachs.

The honeybees return to the hive and pass the nectar onto other worker bees, which suck the nectar from the honeybees' stomachs through their mouths. These "house bees" "chew" the nectar for about half an hour. During this time, enzymes are breaking the complex sugars in the nectar into simple sugars, so that it is both more digestible for the bees and less likely to be attacked by bacteria while stored within the hive.

The bees then spread the nectar throughout the honeycombs where water evaporates from it, making it a thicker syrup. The bees make the nectar dry even faster by fanning it with their wings. Once the honey is gooey enough, the bees seal off the cell of the honeycomb with a plug of wax. The honey is stored until it is eaten. In one year, a colony of bees eats between 120 and 200 pounds of honey.

HOW STUFF WORKS

WHY ONIONS MAKE US CRY.

I'LL BE CRYING, CRYING, CRYING, CRYING YEAH, CRYING, CRYING OVER YOU.

Like other plants, onions are made of cells. These cells are divided into two sections separated by a membrane. One side of the membrane contains a chemical called an enzyme, which helps chemical processes occur in your body. The other side of the membrane contains molecules that contain the element sulfur.

When you cut an onion, the contents on each side of the membrane can mix together freely and the enzyme causes the sulfur compound to undergo a series of chemical reactions. These reactions produce molecules, such as ethylsufine, which make your eyes water.

The products from these reactions are called "transient lives", meaning that they only "live" for a very short time. Their lives are actually so short that scientists are just now learning what they actually are. If you want to prevent crying when you cut onions, there are a few things you can do. One is to cut the onion under a stream of cold water. The sulfur compounds dissolve in water so they will be rinsed down the sink and not be able to get into you eyes.

Another way to prevent crying is to put the onion in the freezer for 10-15 minutes before you cut it. Cold temperatures slow down the reaction between the enzyme and the sulfur compounds, so fewer of the burning molecules can reach your eyes.

2000's

REMEMBER THE 2000'S?
IF NOT, SOMETHING'S WRONG, CUZ THEY'RE STILL HAPPENING.

Thongs
It all started in the late '90's, with a song by Sisqo titled "Thong Song."
A few years later, the thong is the most popular underwear for young
women.

PS2
The Sony Playstation 2 is a hot new game console for gamers.

LiveSTRONG bracelets
Started by champion cyclist Lance Armstrong as a way to raise money for cancer, these yellow wristbands have been sold across the
world and worn as a fashion statement.

Reality Shows
It all started with *Survivor* and *Big Brother*. Along followed others,
such as *Queer Eye for the Straight guy*, *The Simple Life*, *The
Apprentice*, and *The Bachelor*.

MP3 Players
Thanks to filesharing and online music stores, people now upload
most of their music to their MP3 players instead of carrying around
cassettes or CDs.

Napoleon Dynamite
In 2004, this hit movie attracted a cult following. In early 2005, the
search term 'Napoleon Dynamite' was a top phrase searched for
according to Yahoo! and T-Shirts that read, "Vote for Pedro" became
popular among high school and college students.

Suped-Up Cars

After the movie *The Fast and the Furious* was released in 2001, more people started fixing up their cars to make them look better. MTV also released a show called *Pimp My Ride* which takes a beat-up car and remodels it.

Tivo/DVRs (Digital Video Recorders)

With Tivo there are no extra tapes to buy and you can record hours of TV, rewind and playback. On top of all of that, Tivo can remember which types of shows you like just in case you forgot to record something.

Low-Rise Jeans

Jeans that are low at the top and hug the hips.

Camera Phones

Probably the greatest feature ever added to the mobile phone!

TVs and DVD Players for Cars

Thanks to advances in technology, people are able to install DVD players in headrests and flip visors, or install dash monitors so they can watch movies in cars.

Atkins Diet

The popular low-carb diet that everyone tried. It became so popular that even fast food restaraunts were adding Atkins-approved items to their menus.

RETRO GAME

GET FOUR IN A ROW. PLAY AGAINST STRANGER OR FRIEND.
THE WINNER GETS AN ICE CREAM OR A TICKET TO RIO.

RETRO GAME

**GET FOUR IN A ROW. PLAY AGAINST STRANGER OR FRIEND
THE WINNER GETS AN ICE CREAM OR A TICKET TO RIO.**

Popples
These were popular toys in the mid-1980's. Popples were able to pull anything out of their back pouch. The craze was so huge that there was also a cartoon that followed the fad.

Jelly Shoes
If you were a little girl that grew up in the '80's, then chances are you owned a pair of jelly shoes. These were flexible, bright-colored plastic shoes that you could wear without socks.

Slap Bracelets
A flexible metal bracelet with a colorful cloth over it. You would smack these on your wrist and it would wrap around it.

Video Arcades
There are many arcades now, but during the '80s, they were the "in" place to hang out.

Wacky WallWalker
A sticky piece of rubber that usually resembled an insect. You would throw it at a window or wall, and the Wacky Wallwalker would then slowly walk down the surface.

Rubik's Cube
Erno Rubik was looking for a innovative method of teaching his students about 3D objects and came up with what would be called Rubik's Cube. He patented this clever toy and since then 100 million cubes have been sold. The world record for solving the cube is 16.5 seconds!

1980's

REMEMBER THE '80'S?
THIS MIGHT HELP YOU ALONG.

Boom Boxes
Oversized radios were popular with the youth of the early and '80's because they played music so loud, you could hear them from 100 yards away. They eventually came with dual cassette and CD players, and used eight "D" cell batteries to power the big speakers.

Wrestling
Although it has made a comeback in recent years, nothing can compare to the classic years of the WWF and the NWA.

Neon
Pretty self explanatory. Socks, shirts, hair accessories, bracelets, shoe laces, store signs, everything.

Break Dancing
Remember the parachute pants and cardboard boxes that dancers would gyrate on? In 1969, when James Brown was getting down with his big hit "Get on the Good Foot." The Hustle was the big dance style of the day. When he preformed his hit, he did the kind of dance that eventually evolved into break dancing.

Friendship Bracelets
Friendship bracelets came in bright colors, vibrant woven patterns, and had glass beadwork.

Cabbage Patch Dolls
Cabbage Patch Dolls were the doll craze of the '80's, and one of THE fads of the decade.

1980's

**REMEMBER THE '80'S?
THIS MIGHT HELP YOU ALONG.**

Smurfs
Blue elflike creatures, dwelling happily in the forest.

Koosh Balls
During the 1988 Christmas season, the Koosh ball was the hottest toy on the shelves.

'Baby on Board' Signs
Remember when we were supposed to avoid hitting the cars with the 'Baby on Board' signs on them? It's open season on them now.

Trivial Pursuit
We were all playing this board game in the early '80's.

Vans Tennis Shoes
The shoes of choice for skateboarders everywhere.

Hyper-Color Shirts
Shirts that changed color with temperature.

Miami Vice
Pelicans and Ferraris

Hairspray
Big hair was definitly in.

Teenage Mutant Ninja Turtles
A hit cartoon about a bunch of hip turtles who loved eating pizza and could also fight well.

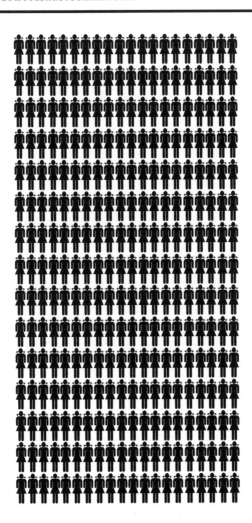

HOW STUFF WORKS

HOW DOES THE INTERNET WORK?

The workhorses of the internet are called "servers." These servers work all night and all day hooked up to a bunch of cables that fling information back and forth. People that request information from these hardworking machines are called "clients." The computer you are on right now is a client that has requested this particular packet of information from a server somewhere. Don't worry. You don't need to tip him.

All or the servers and clients talk to each other through a bunch of straightforward (straightforward for computers, that is) "languages" called protocols. For example, that omnipresent little doohickey "http://" stands for "hypertext transfer protocol," which is how the World Wide Web works. There are other protocols for electronic mail, simple computer file transfers, and many more.

Packets of computer information are sent from computer to computer using numerical addresses called IP addresses. The IP address tells each computer where the packet came from or where it needs to go. An IP address is a series of four numbers connected by dots.

The internet is a worldwide network where all computers use the same language to exchange information.

It is based on a uniform language that is understood by all internet computers: TCP/IP = Transfer Control Protocol/Internet Protocol.

HOW STUFF WORKS

HOW DOES THE INTERNET WORK?

In order to talk to each other, computers use a protocol. A protocol is a language, which can exchange messages (packs of zeros and ones). The computers can understand each other only if they all speak the same language. All computers on the internet and all internet applications, like e-mail, WWW etc. make use of the same language.

A network requires computers that are:

- connected to each other.
- able to talk to each other.

In "classic" networks, computers were mostly connected by means of electric cables. On the internet, the connection can also be made with telephone lines, ISDN, fiberglass, GSM or satellites. Fast connections are called backbones. Their capacity is called bandwidth.

So the next time you go out on the internet, think about all the little people in the computers, talking to each other in the same language, making your visit possible. Hail to the little people.

1970's

Trans Ams
A muscle car that became popular after the movie 'Smokey & the Bandit' which starred Burt Reynolds and Sally Field.

***Star Wars* Action Figures**
After the popular *Star Wars* movies came out, a cult following developed of many fans who couldn't get enough of their favorite characters. Many kids started collecting action figures of Darth Vader, Luke Skywalker, Han Solo and more.

8-Track Tape Players
Developed as a car accessory to give drivers an alternate to listening to radio stations so they could listen to their own song selections. Motorola manufactured the first players, which were installed in Ford automobiles. Many record companies were quick to put many of their artists on the new format, but by the mid 1970's, most record labels had stopped because the quality was poor and they were bulky and inconvenient. Cassette tapes and vinyl records replaced 8-Tracks by the late 1970's.

String Art
Considered to be pop art, this fad was a challenge. You could choose from a variety of unassembled kits ranging from ships to animals. The kits included a board (often covered in black velvet), nails, and enough string that had to be wound around the nails as instructed. They took many hours to complete and could be hung on the wall as a conversation piece.

Cork Pop Guns
When you would shoot it, the cork would pop out and hit your assailant.

1970's

Streakers
People started the craze of taking off all their clothes and running across the field at major sporting events. A streaker ran across the stage of the Oscars in 1973 while it was being broadcast live on TV.

Video Games
The revolution began with Pong in 1972, which spawned Atari (1978) and those little hand-held football games.

Disco Music / Platform Shoes
Saturday Night Fever, ABBA, Donna Summer, The Village People, Dance Fever, Bee Gees. Need we say more?

Dashboard Hula Girls
A small hula girl doll that attached to your car dashboard and danced when the car moved. Made popular by California surfers.

Happy Days/The Fonz
A hit tv show about life in the 1950's. Fonzie was a James Dean type ultra cool guy who rode a motorcycle and could always get a date.

Mexican Jumping Beans
Beans that jump around.

Pet Rocks
More than a million people bought Pet Rocks as Christmas gifts in 1975. Gary Dahl, of Los Gatos, California, got the idea while joking with friends about his easy-to-care-for pet, a rock.

PARANORMAL POWERS

REAL LIFE SUPER HEROES.

Throughout time people have suddenly found they have special abilities. Sometimes, these abilities can be useful, other times they can be downright annoying. Here are some examples of the paranormal powers people have been blessed – or plagued – with.

– Angelo Faticoni was known as the 'human cork.' He could float in the water even with a 20-pound cannonball lashed to his legs.

– Gertrude Smith could make her chickens lay eggs with pictures on them.

– Tom Wiggins, a blind black man who lived in the late 1800's, could flawlessly play any piano piece, no matter how complex, after hearing it performed once or twice. He even copied the exact style of the performer.

– Lulu Hurst never needed karate lessons. Late in the nineteenth century, Hurst had a brief performing career as the 'Georgia Wonder.' The frail 14-year-old could fling three grown men around the stage with no effort, using what she called simply, 'the power.'

– Jaqueline Priestman had so much static electricity in her body that she burned out electrical appliances, and her TV set changed channels whenever she got near it.

– Jenny Morgan had a handshake with a difference. When she shook someone's hand, they would recieve an electric shock that would knock them unconscious.

STAMPS

SAVE SOME MONEY – DESIGN YOUR OWN STAMPS.
PUT THEM ON A LETTER AND SEND TO YOUR FRIENDS.

FUNNY MAN

DRAW A FUNNY MAN!
WELL, ACTUALLY, YOU CAN DRAW FOUR.

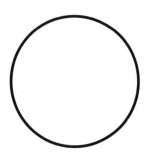

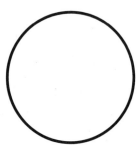

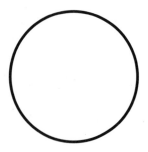

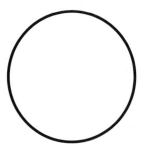

– Peter Strickland's presence made computers and calculators go haywire.

– When physicist Wolfgang Pauli walked into a laboratory, pieces of lab epuipment would tumble off shelves and shatter.

– Benedetto Supino, a nine-year-old Italian boy, had his bed-clothes, furniture and comic books burst into flames when he stared at them.

– In the wake of the accident at the Chernobyl Soviet nuclear power plant, a disturbing number of Russians have reported a newfound ability to make frying pans, irons and silverware stick to their bodies. Some even attract glass and plastic, as well as metal.

– American Frank McKinstry was reportedly so magnetic that if he stood still, his feet stuck to the earth and had to be pried loose.

– A Dutch mystic named Mirin Dajo regularly allowed a sword to be driven through his body with no lasting injury. When skeptics said it must be an illusion, Dajo used an open-ended hollow sword and pumped water through it to show that the entire blade passed through his body. He repeated his daring demonstration some 500 times before he died – as a result of one of the sword wounds.

Paint is made out of two parts, liquid and solid. Some of the liquid part evaporates, that's what you smell when you walk into a freshly painted room.

In liquids, the molecules are weakly attracted to each other. The reason liquids flow is the molecules can slip and slide past each other.

The molecules in solids are strongly attracted to each other, so the molecules cannot slip and slide. As the paint dries, the attractive forces of the remaining molecules increase to form a solid.

However, in modern paint there is an additional process.
As the paint dries, the molecules become so close that the molecules join to form a molecule that is twice the size of the original.
The combining of molecules continues until all are connected to form one huge molecule.

NEW YORK CITY

WEIRD FACTS.

There are 6,374.6 miles of streets in New York City.

The triangular shape of the Flatiron Building (23rd Street) produced wind currents that made women's skirts billow and caused police to create the term '23 skiddoo' to shoo gapers from the area.

Macy's, the world's largest store, covers 2.1 million square feet of space and stocks over 500,000 different items.

As late as the 1840's, thousands of pigs roamed Wall Street to consume garbage – an early sanitation system.

The vaults of the Federal Reserve Bank on Maiden Lane store more than one-quarter of the world's gold bullion.

State muffin (yes, there is a state muffin): the apple muffin

In New York you could eat out every night of your life and never eat at the same restaurant.

The first American chess tournament was held in New York in 1843.

New York City has 722 miles of subway track.

Gennaro Lombardi opened the first United States pizzeria in 1895 in New York City.

EVIL VOODOO DOLL

I TOLD YOU NOT TO TAKE MY PARKING SPACE.

EVIL VOODOO DOLL

SO, YOU'RE SAYING I'M FIRED?

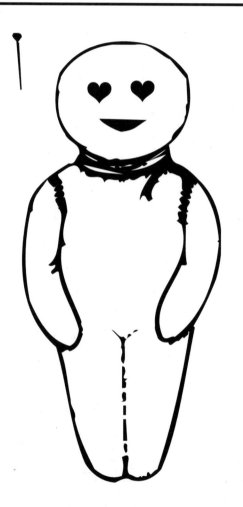

NICE VOODOO DOLL

THAT'S TOO BAD YOU ALREADY HAVE A GIRLFRIEND.
SUCH A SHAME.

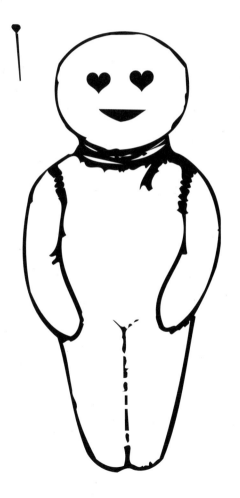

UK-SLANG

– TALK THE TALK

**WE DID NOT INVENT IT, NOR DO WE PROMOTE IT.
BUT IT IS HERE FOR ANYONE EAGER TO USE IT.**

Absobloodylutely - Absolutely

Ace – Excellent, wonderful

Afty – Afternoon. e.g., "Are you going to watch the game this afty?"

Anchors – Brakes. E.g."I slammed the anchors on and hit my head on the steering wheel."

Alright! – Hello. A greeting

Ankle-biters – Children, particularly crawling babies

Argy-bargy – Trouble, noisy quarrelling

As rare as rocking horse shit – Very rare, non existent

Bag – An ugly woman

Ball-ache – A troublesome and inconvenient task, e.g., "Walking 5 miles to and from work, everyday, is a real ball-ache."

Balls(!) – Rubbish, nonsense

Bash – An event, a party. E.g."I'm having a bash at a club for my birthday."

Benny – A tantrum, a fit of anger. "Throw a benny"

Better than a slap in the face with a wet kipper – Expresses that a situation could be considerably worse, hence one should be grateful

Big cheese – A very important person

Big up – To praise, to acclaim

Bingo wings – Fatty, folds of flesh on the underarms of overweight women, who might commonly be seen at Bingo nights.

Blimey(!) – An exclamation of surprise

Bobby – A policeman/woman

Bog off(!) – To go away

Bollocks(!) – Rubbish, nonsense, drivel

Chat up – To talk flirtatiously with someone

Cheeky monkey – A light-hearted name for a verbally impertinent person

Cheers! – 1. Goodbye! – 2. Thank you!

Daft as a brush – Very silly, crazy
Daisies – Boots
Diamond geezer – A really wonderful man, helpful and reliable; a gem of a man

Eh up! – Hello
Egg chasers – Rugby players

The full monty – The complete amount
For Pete's sake! – An exclamation of anger, or frustration
Footy – The game of football

Gaffer – The boss
Geezer – General term for a man

How are you diddling? – A greeting, such as "How do you do?"

In a bit! – Goodbye! See you later!

John Thomas – The penis

Kip – Sleep

Mad for it – Enthusiastic, eager
Mash – To brew a cup of tea

Ow do! – Hello! How do you do!
Old fart – An elderly person
Oh my giddy aunt! – A mild exclamation of surprise

Up and down like a whore's drawers – Said of a person who is unsettled and is unable remain seated and still

Tally-ho! – Goodbye
Tacky – Of poor taste, lacking style

Wanker – An idiot, an incompetent person

MONKEYS

HOW MANY MONKEYS CAN YOU FIND? THE ANSWER IS ON PAGE 219 OF THE DETROIT METROPOLITAN PHONE DIRECTORY.

SPEECH

THIS TIME IT'S GONG TO HAPPEN. I CAN FEEL IT.

Write your acceptance speech now, s
when you win the Oscar, you don't
have to stand there like a
moron, fumbling with a
piece of paper.

Name:

**STARBUCKS - TAKEN! COCA COLA - TAKEN! IKEA - TAKEN!
MAKE SURE YOU THINK OF SOMETHNG UNIQUE.**

Business idea!
This is how I'm gonna make my first million:

ON THE PHONE

LET YOUR PEN LOOSE.
FILL IN THE FIRES.

ON THE PHONE

LET YOUR PEN LOOSE.
FILL IN THE HEARTS.

ON THE PHONE

LET YOUR PEN LOOSE.
FILL IN THE GIRAFFES AND FLOWERS.

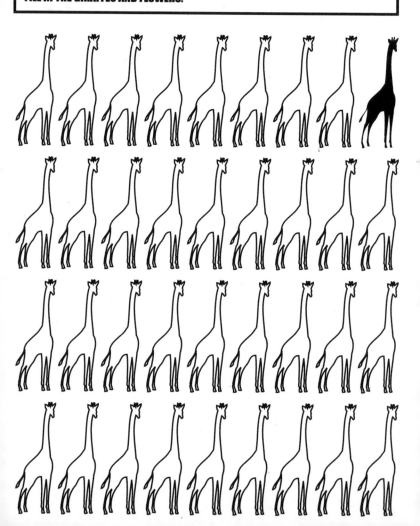

MY NOTES

OK, FOLKS. SO, I GUESS NOW WE'RE DONE.
TIME IS WASTED AND WE'VE HAD A GOOD TIME.
BUT JUST BECAUSE WE ARE DONE THERE IS NO NEED TO
GO BACK TO THE SAME OLD, BORING LIFE. NO, NO.
KEEP WASTING TIME. JUST REMEMBER,
WHATEVER YOU DO, DO IT WITH STYLE.

BAAH! BAAH!

CHECK IT OUT!

WWW.URBANOUTFITTERS.COM
WWW.NICOTEXT.COM

WWW.URBANOUTFITTERS.COM WWW.NICOTEXT.COM CHECK IT OUT! WWW.URBANOUTFITTERS.COM WWW.NICOTEXT.COM WWW.NICOTEXT.COM CHECK IT OUT! WWW.URBANOUTFITTERS.COM WWW.NICOTEXT.COM CHECK IT OUT! WWW.URBANOUTFITTERS.COM WWW.NICOTEXT.COM CHECK IT OUT! WWW.URBANOUTFITTERS.COM WWW.NICOTEXT.COM CHECK IT OUT! WWW.URBANOUTFITTERS.COM WWW.NICOTEXT.COM CHECK IT OUT! WWW.URBANOUTFITTERS.COM WWW.NICOTEXT.COM CHECK IT OUT! WWW.URBANOUTFITTERS.COM WWW.NICOTEXT.COM CHECK IT OUT! WWW.URBANOUTFITTERS.COM WWW.NICOTEXT.COM CHECK IT OUT! WWW.URBANOUTFITTERS.COM WWW.NICOTEXT.COM CHECK IT OUT! WWW.URBANOUTFITTERS.COM WWW.NICOTEXT.COM CHECK IT OUT! WWW.URBANOUTFITTERS.COM WWW.NICOTEXT.COM CHECK IT OUT! WWW.URBANOUTFITTERS.COM WWW.NICOTEXT.COM CHECK IT OUT! WWW.URBANOUTFITTERS.COM WWW.NICOTEXT.COM CHECK IT OUT! WWW.URBANOUTFITTERS.COM WWW.NICOTEXT.COM CHECK IT OUT! WWW.URBANOUTFITTERS.COM WWW.NICOTEXT.COM CHECK IT OUT! WWW.URBANOUTFITTERS.COM WWW.NICOTEXT.COM CHECK IT OUT! WWW.URBANOUTFITTERS.COM WWW.NICOTEXT.COM CHECK IT OUT! WWW.URBANOUTFITTERS.COM WWW.NICOTEXT.COM CHECK IT OUT! WWW.URBANOUTFITTERS.COM WWW.NICOTEXT.COM WWW.NICOTEXT.COM CHECK IT OUT! WWW.URBANOUTFITTERS.COM WWW.NICOTEXT.COM CHECK IT OUT!